To those who love and
serve vulnerable children

And God is able to
bless you abundantly,
so that in all things
at all times,
having all that you need,
you will abound
in every good work.

— 2 CORINTHIANS 9:8 —

Presence Matters

A 40-DAY JOURNEY INTO THE RELATIONSHIP BETWEEN
Faith, Science & Trauma

BETH GUCKENBERGER

iDisciple | Publishing

Foreword

"You must meet Beth Guckenberger. She and her husband Todd have an amazing family full of birth and adopted kids and a worldwide ministry to orphan and vulnerable children."

Two years after we heard these words, we had the opportunity to meet Beth and Todd. In 2014, we joined the staff of Back2Back Ministries to share our expertise in trauma-informed training. We experienced firsthand Beth's genuine heart, love for kids, and deep desire to be a healer in the lives of children and teens. One of the most remarkable things about Beth is that she is fully present when you have a conversation with her. She is not distracted by her heavy responsibilities, phone calls, or beeping text messages. We can't think of a better person to be the author of a book entitled *Presence Matters*.

We celebrate the release of this book written by Beth and the Trauma Free World team because it is one of a kind. Throughout this book, they share practical, life-giving strategies for how to be a healing presence in the life of a child, teen, or even adult. This 40-day journey will enable you to experience how faith and science work together to bring hope to a wounded heart. God's Word is full of trauma-informed principles, and *Presence Matters* connects those principles to scientific, evidence-based solutions. It is transformational to realize science is catching up with what God has told us all along.

Not only will you experience how faith and science have something to say about healing from trauma, but you will also see yourself in these pages. In our journey into trauma-informed ministries, we have learned that many of us who are helping others need help ourselves. This book is an encouragement to look at ourselves and become keenly aware of the needs of our own hearts.

We've discovered in the years we have been doing this work that the more we dig into the impact of trauma, the more compassion we have for the hurting. Yet without the many tools shared in this book, we won't have the competency to do the work we are called to do.

This book will change you. It changed us. You will see yourself differently, and, perhaps for the first time, visit wounds from your past and experience healing. You will see those in your world differently as you understand their challenges in dealing with adverse childhood experiences. And, you will see our Heavenly Father differently as you experience His heart of compassion for the vulnerable and hurting.

You will put this book down once you have ended the journey, but we believe you will refer to it repeatedly as people in your life need the same help it brought you.

David Schooler, Th. D. , pastor, and counselor

Jayne Schooler, Co-author of *Wounded Children, Healing Homes; Telling the Truth to Your Foster or Adopted Children;* and *The Whole Life Adoption Book*

Presence Matters
Copyright 2022

Unless otherwise indicated, all Scripture quotations are taken from the *New American Standard Bible,* ® copyright ©1960, 1962, 1963, 1968, 1971, 1972, 1973, 1975, 1977, 1995 by *The Lockman Foundation.* Used by permission.

Scripture quotations marked *NIV* are taken from the *Holy Bible, New International Version,*® *NIV.* ® Copyright © 1973,1978, 1984, 2011 by *Biblica, Inc.*® Used by permission. All rights reserved worldwide.

Scripture quotations marked *NLT* are taken from the *Holy Bible, New Living Translation,* copyright © 1996, 2004, 2015 by *Tyndale House Foundation.* Used by permission of *Tyndale House Publishers, Inc.*, Carol Stream, Illinois 60188. All rights reserved.

Scripture quotations marked *KJV* are takenfrom the *Holy Bible, King James Version.*

Scripture quotations marked *ESV* are taken from *The Holy Bible, English Standard Version*® *(ESV®),* copyright © 2001 by *Crossway,* a publishing ministry of *Good News Publishers.* Used by permission. All rights reserved.

Published by iDisciple Publishing

2555 Northwinds Parkway, Alpharetta GA 30009

ISBN: 9780578337371

Presence Matters

TABLE OF
Contents

"I have told you these things, so that in me you may have peace.
In this world you will have trouble.
But take heart! I have overcome the world. "

— JOHN 16:33 —

Week One

The Trouble of This World Matters

Jesus said we *will* have trouble and He was right. The world around us—maybe even the story we live in—is full of hurt, pain, and suffering. Wouldn't it be something if life turned out the way we planned? We would likely remove the parts of our story that involve pain and suffering and yet it's often in those places that God transforms our hearts and draws us in.

Of the two billion children in the world, one billion experience the effects of trauma. That is one out of every two children!

Yet we *"take heart!"* because…

> Jesus has overcome the world.
> There are five billion adults in the world who can rally around hurting children.
> Resources, research, and training exist for hope and healing.

This week we will learn about the impact of trauma and begin the transformational journey of recognizing and responding to pain in a way that brings the compassion and healing of Christ.

Presence Matters

The steadfast love of the Lord never ceases; his mercies never come to an end; they are new every morning; great is your faithfulness.

— LAMENTATIONS 3:22–23 (ESV)

William, the victim of domestic abuse, is removed from his home and now navigates a new environment with the added weight of emotional pain and separation from the members of his family. It has to be this way but doesn't seem fair. The fallout is poor sleep, lack of concentration in school, skittishness around new adults, withdrawal, and low-grade depression. He is wondering if anyone even cares anymore, and his overall feeling is *desperation.*

Juanita's cancer diagnosis arrives without warning and disrupts her life and plans. Everyone in her family pays a price. Juanita has physical pain and battles against a disease. Her children struggle with feelings of confusion and frustration as they fight one another for any leftover attention, and Juanita's husband attempts to hold it all together. This wasn't how they saw life unfolding. It's unfair. The family is vulnerable and hurting, and their overall feeling is *despair.*

Cecilia is neglected at home and seemingly overlooked at school. Only 10 years old, she thinks, *What is so wrong with me that no one cares?* Hungry for care, she thrives under the attention of an "uncle" and submits to his uncomfortable advances. *I can't lose him too,* she rationalizes. Emotionally disconnecting her body from her mind, she floats above her circumstances until she simply forgets where she is. Her overall feeling is *emptiness.*

Emotional abuse. Physical abuse. Trauma. Sexual abuse. Racism. Neglect. Suffering. Abandonment. Violence. Exploitation. These realities are a part of the human

experience. We can work to mitigate their effect and impact the systems that set up these cruelties, but still, many will experience them.

Why does Jesus let this happen?
What is He doing as He sees it unfolding?
What should our response be?

The chief response of Jesus to suffering is compassion. It drives Him to:

- Heal the sick (Matt. 14:14).
- Feed the hungry (Matt. 15:32).
- Teach the crowds (Mark 6:34).
- Wipe away the tears of the bereaved (Luke 7:13).

The Greek word for compassion (*splagchnizomai*) is the same in each of these verses. It's translated as "to be moved down to one's bowels." Jesus' compassion reaches deep down into His guts, rises up within Him, and compels Him to action.

We read twice in the Gospels that Jesus wept, both times in response to the suffering of another. In John 11, He weeps over the death of His friend, Lazarus, and in Luke 19, He cries for Jerusalem. He felt deeply, and since we are made in His image, we do too.

When we allow ourselves to be moved by the pain of another, we model Christ's compassion and character. The Hebrew word *ra'ah* meaning "to see" also means "to respond to a need." Embedded in the definition of this ancient word is a question: If we don't do anything about what we see, have we really looked at someone? Compassion can and should move us… to listen, fight for, come alongside, or offer ourselves on behalf of others. No matter how empathy wells up in our guts, may it cause us to reach out and connect, knowing in the end that *presence matters*.

Trauma-informed Tip

The first step to becoming trauma-informed is awareness. We must "see" and acknowledge the existence of trauma and its impact on people around us—our neighbor, the person sitting next to us in church, even those within our own homes. When we witness a difficult circumstance or find ourselves in the middle of a hard story, we need to open our eyes to the events taking place. Only then can we respond with the compassion of Christ.

1. When I am in the midst of suffering, what do I picture God doing at that time (e.g., shaking His finger at me, not paying attention, crying with me...)?
2. What truth about the love and compassion of God is hard for me to believe?
3. When overwhelmed by stress or pain, what is one way I can connect with God?

_____

_____

_____

_____

_____

_____

_____

_____

_____

_____

_____

_____

_____

_____

_____

_____

_____

_____

_____

_____

_____

_____

_____

_____

Prayer

Jesus, help us to have eyes to see and a heart to respond to those who hurt.
We want to show Your compassion to a brokenhearted world. Amen.

Trauma Is a Thief

Be sober-minded; be watchful. Your adversary the devil
prowls around like a roaring lion, seeking someone to devour.
— 1 PETER 3:8 (ESV)

At 18 years old, Eunice experienced an unexpected pregnancy, causing her to float between friends' couches, no longer welcome in her parents' house. The stress of working two jobs and paying bills was more than she knew how to handle. She often wished the baby growing inside her would just disappear. She even tried once to free herself from the pregnancy, punching her stomach until it left black and blue bruises. But the little baby still wiggled and hiccupped inside of her. When her due date arrived, the birth was complicated, and without access to quality medical care, she nearly bled out. Even before his birth, Eunice and her new son, Lamonte, had experienced significant trauma.

As a new mom, Eunice needed money for diapers and formula. Lacking choices, she would leave Lamonte home alone for hours while she worked, although always with toys, snacks, and a blanket. As far as she could tell, it was working; Lamonte never seemed to cry. Knowing the boy was being left alone for hours, the neighbors called children's services and Eunice watched in shock as the social worker rushed her baby to the hospital while yelling about "dehydration." Eunice was soon informed her son would be placed in foster care and her immediate thought was, *He's probably better off without me.*

Now a teenager, Lamonte wonders about his mother and why she hadn't wanted him. He struggles in school and often skips classes for days at a time. He's a regular drug user and scares himself with how often he turns to alcohol. People comment that he "has a chip on his shoulder" and "should be grateful for the people who take care of him." What they don't know is that there have been a *lot* of them—18 different foster homes, 18 different "parents" telling him in one way or another to "grow up" and "act his age." Lamonte finally decides he is better off alone and keeps people in his life at arm's length.

Trauma is passed down from one generation to the next. It's being repeated, in one form or another, in hundreds of millions of lives every day. It's the effect of living in a broken and fallen world.

Trauma is the work of a thief who comes to steal and kill and destroy the world God intended for goodness, beauty, and life to the full (John 10:10). It steals physical, emotional, and psychological safety. It kills permanency and predictability and destroys well-being, derailing all areas of development.

And trauma's destructive reach doesn't stop there. In some cases...

- The brain develops differently and struggles to process memory, emotions, language and judgment. [1]
- The body's development is delayed, impacting growth, illness, the senses, and even genetic expression. [2]
- Belief systems are warped to include thoughts like "I'm damaged," "I'm powerless," or "I'm worthless."
- Behavior becomes unpredictable, disruptive, and fear-based.[3]
- Relationships are characterized by an inability to trust or to set healthy boundaries. [4]

Yet there is hope, because trauma is *not the end of the story*.

God is not wringing His hands wondering what to do with this mess. He is actively at work right this moment. He equips His people with the compassion and resources to bring hope, restoration, and healing.

God is inviting us to be a part of the stories of hope and redemption He is writing in the darkest of places. Even the darkness is not dark to Him (Psalm 139:1–2).

Trauma-informed Tip

The first goal of a person who is becoming trauma-informed is to understand the life-altering impact of trauma. Trauma can, especially in early childhood, impact the brain and typical development. A child's chronological age and developmental stage may not be in sync.[5] A child might be *chronologically* 10-years-old but *developmentally* is more like a five-, six-, or seven-year-old. So, to avoid frustration for both you and the child, set your expectations so they are aligned with a child's *developmental* age.

1. Where in my life or the life of someone I know have I seen trauma? What might have been its impact?
2. In what ways have I seen God's light in circumstances that felt dark? How did I know it was Him?
3. What behaviors do I see in someone else that could be the result of trauma in their life?

_____
_____
_____
_____
_____
_____
_____
_____
_____
_____
_____
_____
_____
_____
_____
_____
_____
_____
_____
_____
_____
_____
_____

Prayer

Lord, we are so grateful for Your healing power. Give us hope to believe we can reach for Your light in the midst of darkness. Amen.

When We Feel Safe

For you did not receive the spirit of slavery to fall back into fear, but you have received the Spirit of adoption as sons, by whom we cry, "Abba! Father!"

— ROMANS 8:15 (ESV)

Gloria had never been to a real restaurant before—one with menus, waiters, and unfamiliar foods. No matter how much her foster parents explained what it would be like, Gloria felt anxious.

When it was time for bed, Gloria stared at the ceiling, her mind racing with thoughts about what tomorrow might bring. *How could they make her do this?* The ball of fearful anxiety in Gloria's stomach began to turn into the armor of anger and frustration. *They always do what they want to do, not what I want to do.* Gloria's anger drove her out of bed and straight into her foster mom's room. Gloria shouted, "I'm not going to that stupid restaurant tomorrow! I don't want to go anywhere with you people! You can't make me!"

When people feel safe, they have access to all parts of their brain, including an area called the prefrontal cortex, which helps us learn, use logic and reason, and predict how our actions might affect someone else.

Since the world we live in is not always safe, God designed our brains with an incredible capacity for protection. When we feel threatened by something or someone, the brain "shuts down" parts of itself—most importantly, the prefrontal cortex—in order to save energy for more important activities, like staying alive! This state is often referred to as the "fear brain," and it instinctively reacts to perceived threats with a "fight, flight, or freeze" response. In that moment, we're either going to attack the threat head on, run away from it, or freeze, unable to do anything.

This is important for those of us who are growing in our awareness of the effects of trauma. When children live in constantly chaotic and unsafe environments, their brains are in a *chronic* state of fear. It's like a gear shift that gets stuck; even if the environment and circumstances change, the brain is unable to shift back to a healthy state.

Living in the *fear brain* looks like:

- A suppressed conscience, unable to distinguish right from wrong
- Little access to higher level thinking, planning, and reasoning
- Use of protective strategies like manipulation, triangulation, and aggression that prevent healthy relationships
- An inability or unwillingness to express one's needs
- An inability to discern the needs of others
- A heightened startle response
- A quick, sometimes irrational, shift into fight, flight, or freeze

God is well acquainted with the effects of fear. He knows how unhealthy levels of fear can disable the well-designed function of the human brain. But He hasn't left us defenseless!

For God hath not given us the spirit of fear; but of power, and of love, and of a sound mind.
— 2 TIMOTHY 1:7 (KJV)

We know both from Scripture and experience that a spirit of fear stands in direct opposition to a sound mind. It depletes our power and stifles our capacity to love. It's why God is graciously persistent in offering us His perfect peace and protection. He longs for us to find our safety and security in Him. When we do, our brain is able to relax, having full access to all of its incredible capabilities. How beautiful! When we recognize fear and invite the peace of God into our lives and into the lives of those around us, we are empowered to be part of God's redemptive work in this broken and disintegrated world.

Trauma-informed Tip

Learning the signs of the fear brain is key to a trauma-informed response. Look for:
- An inability to discern right from wrong
- An inability to voice needs or recognize needs in others
- A quick or irrational reaction of fight, flight, or freeze
- Dilated pupils
- A tense body or clenched jaw
- An increase in the startle response

When you recognize these signs of fear in yourself or others, make a plan to increase feelings of peace and safety. Pray for God's peace, practice deep breathing, give or gather more information, or minimize other stress or distractions.

1. When I am afraid, is my natural tendency to attack the threat head on, run away from it, or freeze where I am?
2. How have I experienced God's peace in the middle of a fearful situation?
3. What are three ways I can feel safe when I am afraid? What are three ways I can help people around me feel safe when they are afraid?

_____

_____

_____

_____

_____

_____

_____

_____

_____

_____

_____

_____

_____

_____

_____

_____

_____

_____

_____

_____

Prayer

*Jesus, we don't want to be afraid. Give us courage and
confidence to face our past hurts and unknown futures. Amen.*

Lay Down Your Weapons

"The Lord will fight for you; you need only to be still."
— EXODUS 14:14

When a soldier goes into battle, he takes a weapon—a sharp sword, a loaded gun, a ready shield. In the face of an enemy, he needs something to defend himself and ward off the inevitable attack. Without protection, he is vulnerable and unlikely to survive.

Eric knows weapons are essential for survival. He knows the feeling of terror that surges to the surface anytime he feels exposed and vulnerable. But Eric isn't a soldier. He's a fifteen-year-old boy, and his fight is waged at home and has been for as long as he can remember.

It starts when Dad walks through the door. Eric never knows what to expect. Will his dad be the kind and loving father that jokes and plays basketball, or the angry and violent drunk with a short temper and quick fists? Eric has to be on guard, ready to hit back, to respond with his own rage, to *survive*.

Sometimes Eric pits his parents against each other. If he can stir up conflict between them, they fight with each other, keeping Eric and his younger sisters out of harm's way. He would rather watch them attack one another than suffer an attack himself or, worse, watch them attack the girls. Every day is a battle, and he's determined to survive. His weapons are:

- Manipulation
- Violence
- Control
- Triangulation
- Aggression
- Lying

These natural responses to extreme fear are called "protection strategies."[6] As adults, we might label them "poor behavior" and tell a kid to stop being violent or manipulative or controlling. We forget these weapons are useful and protective strategies. With our "stop," we rip the weapons out of their hands, leaving them exposed and vulnerable. Instead, our job is to communicate, "This is a safe place to lay your weapons down. You won't need them here."

When we picture a scared child hiding behind the shield of control and the sword of violence, suddenly a new opportunity emerges to exchange weapons for tools.

- "Instead of control or violence, use the tool of your voice and ask for what you need. I promise I will listen to you."

- "Instead of the weapon of manipulation, use the tool of a negotiation and ask for a compromise."

Rather than stripping away the only weapons a child or teen has ever used to survive, we can make an exchange.

Fear provokes the pulling out of weapons. It's why God repeatedly tells us not to fear, we are His, and He will do the fighting.

"He will never leave you nor forsake you. Do not be afraid; do not be discouraged."
— DEUTERONOMY 31:8

"Fear not, for I have redeemed you; I have called you by name; you are mine."
— ISAIAH 43:1 (ESV)

He knows that when we are fearful, our natural response is to reach for our fear-driven weapons. When we do, we end up looking more like our enemy than like God. He teaches in His Word that it's safe to lay down our weapons, to release the old sinful strategies we've used to protect ourselves and to learn the new tools of the Kingdom.

Trauma-informed Tip

When you see a child or teen using a protection strategy (i.e., manipulation, violence, lying, aggression, control, or triangulation), ask yourself, *What are they afraid of?* Increase felt safety by relaxing your own body, speaking in a calming voice, and lowering yourself below their eye level. Even sitting quietly in a child's presence can calm them. Proactively teach new tools like how to ask for something with respect or to ask for a compromise. Then, gently remind them to use the tools they have already learned.

1. When I feel unsafe or insecure, which weapons do I reach for?
2. What is one truth about God I can depend on to believe He is fighting for me?
3. What are one or two phrases I can use to redirect a kid or teen toward understanding they are safe and don't need their weapon?

Lord, if I am going to be calm and curb my natural response, I need You to give me grace. Grant me patience and self-control and fill me with the fruits of Your Spirit. Amen.

Mindfulness Is about Presence

You keep him in perfect peace whose mind is stayed on you, because he trusts in you.
— ISAIAH 26:3 (ESV)

On John's first day of work, the community center was buzzing with the noise and activity of children laughing, soccer balls flying, and adults trying to maintain peace amidst 50 rambunctious kids. Knowing his first goal was to connect and build relationships, John looked around to find someone to engage. He was overwhelmed and unsure where to begin, so he took out his guitar to calm his nerves. As he lightly played a melody, he noticed for the first time a quiet teenage boy, Tyler, in the corner. John noticed the way Tyler tapped his fingers to the melody. He asked the other adults about the boy and heard, "He doesn't want to be here", "He's kind of a loner", and "He's really serious."

Undeterred, John crossed the room, introduced himself, and offered to teach Tyler to play a few chords. Although he was hesitant, Tyler took the guitar and strummed his first chords. This was the moment things in his life began to change.

In just a few short months, Tyler transformed from the quiet teen in the corner to a confident one onstage with the worship band at his church. John's consistent presence and encouragement spurred him to develop his talent. This story has a dramatic ending, but a quiet beginning; it was John's mindfulness that kindled the first spark.

Mindfulness can be a confusing word. Ultimately, mindfulness is about presence. It's an active engagement in your present reality, allowing you to be aware of your own needs and emotions and the needs and emotions of those around you.

John was overwhelmed by the chaos of the community center and felt nervous and out of place. He was mindful of those emotions and used his guitar to focus on his present reality. In doing so, he saw the people around him, including Tyler, alone and isolated in the corner.

We see Jesus exercise mindfulness in Luke chapter 5. On His way to heal a sick child, He and His disciples are surrounded by an overwhelming crowd of people clamoring for His attention. In the middle of all of the chaos, Jesus is present and aware. He stops everyone as He feels the "power go out of him." A broken, hurting, and rejected woman had snuck through the crowd to touch just the hem of His garment. In spite of the chaos and the very important thing He was about to do, Jesus was present enough to sense her touch, stop what He was doing, honor her, and heal her.

Jesus is just as mindful of you and me today. Psalm 8:4 says, "*What is mankind that you are mindful of them, human beings that you care for them?*"

- Jesus is aware of and attuned to your needs.
- He is not overwhelmed or distracted by the chaos of this world.
- He is deeply engaged in your present reality, ready to pursue you, and ready to meet your need for healing.

When we are mindful of the needs and emotions bubbling up inside of us, we can take steps to calm down and come back to our present reality. Once we are calm, we are able to look around and become aware of others in a way that looks like Jesus and opens the door for healing.

Trauma-informed Tip

Take regular time to pause during the day and assess how the world and its chaos is impacting you. Start with a one-minute timer on your phone and mentally scan your body and heart for areas of distraction or tension. First, bring your mind to your present reality. Then, look for the needs of those around you.

1. What are three things that make it hard to slow down or be mindful (e.g., social media, a full schedule, kids, work...)?
2. During times of rest or intentional focus, how have I noticed God tending to my needs?
3. What is one way my lack of mindfulness has negatively impacted someone around me? What is one way my use of mindfulness could positively impact someone around me?

_____

_____

_____

_____

_____

_____

_____

_____

_____

_____

_____

_____

_____

_____

_____

_____

_____

_____

_____

_____

_____

Prayer

*Jesus, I want to stay fixed on You. I want my thoughts on You,
and to believe Your thoughts are on me. Keep me mindful. Amen.*

This week, what did I learn about myself? Others? The Lord?

_____

_____

_____

_____

_____

_____

_____

_____

_____

_____

_____

_____

_____

_____

_____

_____

_____

_____

_____

_____

_____

_____

_____

"God sets the lonely in families..."

— **PSALM 68:6** —

Week Two

Relationships Matter

God's answer to loneliness, abandonment, and trauma is relationship. This doesn't always mean family (although a safe family has always been God's intention), but it will always include a community and a place to belong. Being connected in safe relationships is essential for healing.

This week we will look at why relationships matter, how they shape our past, present, and future, and how they are divinely designed by the One who calls us into connection.

A Willingness To Be Known

He has shown you, O mortal, what is good. And what does the LORD require of
you? To act justly and to love mercy and to walk humbly with your God.

— MICAH 6:8

A leader in a local community center put a creative spin on a simple technique for helping children notice and share their emotions. The technique, as it's widely used, is to ask a child the question, *"How's your heart (or engine) running?"*[7] In response, the child can move a dial on a paper plate speedometer to blue for "too slow", red for "too fast", or green if they are feeling calm.

Knowing this system but wanting to contextualize it for his group, the community leader used basketballs to help his students share their emotions. As each kid walked through the door, he asked, "How's your heart running?" If their heart was running fast that day, they shot a red basketball. If their heart was running slow, they shot a blue one. And if they were emotionally comfortable, they shot a green basketball.

This simple check-in gave each student a way to communicate to their peers and the other adults in the room, without even needing words. And it made it easy for the adults to ask follow-up questions like, *"Hey, why did you shoot red today?"* *"What is making today go well for you?"* Or, *"What's dragging you down?"* Questions like these build interdependence and help relationships grow. As relationships are established, needs can be communicated and practical expressions of God's love can be shared.

Just before his death, Jesus gave his disciples one powerful instruction. He said,

"A new command I give you: Love one another… By this everyone will know that you are my disciples, if you love one another"

— JOHN 13:34–35

In the years that followed, we see how literally the disciples took this command. They cared for widows and orphans. They reached out to the slave, the hungry, the sick. They intimately knew and cared for vulnerable people, and, in return, those people became curious about Jesus of Nazareth and His teaching. House churches flourished as communities cared for one another. Four centuries later, Christianity was the dominant faith in the Asia Minor region. God's plan works.

Today, we are called to do the same thing—draw near to vulnerable people. Like the community leader who created a way to check in with his students, we must be willing to put in the time and use every available technique to connect with and care for those around us who are hurting. Professional counseling, mentorship, scholarship programs, tutoring, financial training, and other resources can help, but a gap remains—one that can only be filled by the presence of someone who loves and cares well.

Trauma-informed Tip

A creative check-in routine can make it easier to connect with a child or teen who may need help expressing their emotions.[8] If necessary, use props or a game to jumpstart communication.

1. How have I seen God's love for me through someone else? What can I do today to thank them and thank God?
2. Which emotions are easy for me to talk about with others? Which are hard to share?
3. Who have I seen consistently draw near to vulnerable people? What can I learn from their example?

_____
_____
_____
_____
_____
_____
_____
_____
_____
_____
_____
_____
_____
_____
_____
_____
_____
_____
_____
_____

Prayer

Jesus, I want to be known as Your disciple by the love I share with others.
Help me connect with and care for those around me in need. Amen.

Looking for Someone Who's Looking for Him

"The LORD does not look at the things people look at.
People look at the outward appearance, but the LORD looks at the heart."
— 1 SAMUEL 16:7

Dev's cry pierced the quiet night as he made his way to the front door, attempting to get outside. His adoptive mom came behind him, slowly patting his back. His loud cries turned to small hiccups as she led Dev back to his room. She prayed he'd find comfort in his new home and with his new family.

The adoption of three-year-old Dev was finalized only months prior. His first weeks with new people consisted largely of severe emotional breakdowns. When the adoption agency handed over his file, it didn't contain many details. There was no medical history, no timeline of previous placements, and no information on his biological parents—just a simple paragraph describing the store where he was found wandering when picked up by children's services.

His adoptive parents realized quickly he would need a different kind of care than their three biological children. When they were three years old, Salud and RJ's other children could speak in full sentences, follow directions, and climb the jungle gym. Dev, however, was clumsy, seemingly not picking up his feet when he walked. He spoke words like "water" and "cookie," but mostly used gestures. They liked to say they were all "learning to speak Dev". When they couldn't figure out what he needed, he was inconsolable.

Relationship was uncomfortable, yet relationship is *exactly* what Dev needed to heal.

Salud and RJ had to let go of their expectations of what a child his age needed or could accomplish and learned to ask instead, "What does *our* three-year-old need?" This required slowing down their schedules to focus on Dev. They kept him close and moved a rocking chair into his room so Salud could rock him to sleep. They bought toys appropriate for a one-year-old and engaged him in play using all of his senses.

Wrapped in this warm and nurturing environment, Dev began to heal. In just a few months, he was speaking full sentences, surprising them with at least one new word a day. His coordination improved and his inconsolable fits were less frequent. On his fifth birthday, his parents marveled as he confidently blew out his candles and ran to play with friends. For Dev, relationships changed everything.

> *"Every child is born looking for someone who is looking for him."*
> — DR. CURT THOMPSON

The presence of a safe adult and the emotional quality of our earliest relationships have the greatest influence on human development.[9] Relationships are so powerful that they set a child on either a healthy or unhealthy trajectory. Nowhere is this more evident than in God's design of the human body. Babies are fully dependent on their primary caregiver to meet their needs. Nearly every system in the human body is dependent on interaction with another person to develop in a healthy way.

We are designed by God to develop, grow, and thrive by living in the context of healthy relationships. This should come as no surprise since we are all created in the image of God, who—as Father, Son, and Spirit—models perfect relationship. God invites every person into relationship with Him, just as Jesus lived in relationship with others while on Earth. He commissioned the disciples in pairs (Mark 6:7) and prior to ascending into heaven, prayed for unity among believers (John 17:22–23).

There is no exception. God's consistent plan for growth, healing, and flourishing is through relationship with Him and relationships with one another.

Trauma-informed Tip

Deep and healthy relationships are fostered through consistency. This is especially true for those who've experienced trauma. So it's important to limit changes in caregivers and other adults (like teachers, tutors, or mentors) and to simplify schedules and eliminate distractions in order to prioritize connection time.

1. What does my relationship with God look like? How does consistency impact my connection with God?
2. How have relationships (either good or bad) shaped my life?
3. Who in my life needs a positive relationship? What can I do to make them feel invited into healthy relationship?

_____

_____

_____

_____

_____

_____

_____

_____

_____

_____

_____

_____

_____

_____

_____

_____

_____

_____

_____

_____

Prayer

Jesus, You desire that we would all be in relationship with You.
Help me think and prioritize in terms of relationship. Amen.

He Runs To Us

The people will be secure in their land. They will know that I am the Lord, when I
break the bars of their yoke and rescue them from the hands of those who enslaved them.

— EZEKIEL 34: 27

Teenaged Jason "borrowed" a car without permission and without a license. "I can't believe you would go behind my back like that," his foster mom Karla rants. "I can't trust you and you repeatedly show me disrespect. You are never going to change! There is no hope for you."

As she storms out of the room still talking under her breath, Jason feels frustrated. He honestly wasn't thinking about her when he took the car. "It wasn't personal," he wants to say. Karla can be heard from the other room, muttering about not knowing what to do anymore. Jason defends himself to no one in particular, saying she wouldn't understand, and, since no one got hurt, what is the big deal?

Jason's one act suddenly has the relationship in jeopardy. In her stress and fear, Karla judges her son and forecasts his future as hopeless rather than using the opportunity to better understand him. With the relationship at risk, Jason feels shame and Karla feels despair.

How could this situation turn around and be used as an opportunity for healing?

It starts with understanding God's choice to pursue relationship with us instead of revenge, punishment, or retaliation. When we make poor decisions, He doesn't shake His head at us or take it personally. Instead, He uses it as a chance to demonstrate grace. When we grasp the grace God extends to us, we have increased capacity to extend it to others.

In Luke 15, the story of the Prodigal Son, the father sets an example of parenting with a relationship-first mindset. The younger of his two sons boldly demands his share of the inheritance, insinuating that life would be better if his father were dead. Despite valid reasons this father could be offended, he grants it.

What follows is a series of bad choices by the younger son, and when he finally heads home, the shame and guilt heavy on his shoulders, he is met with an unexpected response.

> *"But while he was still a long way off, his father saw him and felt compassion, and ran and embraced him and kissed him. And the son said to him, 'Father, I have sinned against heaven and before you. I am no longer worthy to be called your son.' But the father said to his servants, 'Bring quickly the best robe, and put it on him, and put a ring on his hand, and shoes on his feet. And bring the fattened calf and kill it, and let us eat and celebrate. For this my son was dead, and is alive again; he was lost, and is found.' And they began to celebrate."*
>
> — LUKE 15:20–24 (ESV)

While he was still *a long way off*, the father went to the son... before he was cleaned up and repentant and before he had proved that he had "learned his lesson."

Even though the father had every right to be angry, he initiated reconciliation. He chose the boy over all else and put that on display for his community. This is how the Father loves us. He sent His Son to "run to us" while we were still far off, knowing that in relationship and connection, we find healing.

When we face bad behavior from a child or teen, it's an opportunity to look like our Father and pursue relationship over all else. It doesn't have to be lavish, just a simple invitation to try again.

For Karla, that means asking Jason if she can have a "re-do"—a chance to hear his side of the story. While they are both calm, Karla teaches Jason rather than jumping straight to punishment. It's not easy, but the result is that their relationship is preserved so Jason can continue to find love and healing in Karla's home.

Trauma-informed Tip

When you see a child or teen behaving badly, look beyond the behavior and establish connection. This may mean taking a few deep breaths and reminding yourself of the grace God has given you and the opportunity you have to extend grace to others. Rather than relying on common disconnecting responses like "Go to your room", try a connecting response like, "Let's sit together and talk this out", or "Let's go for a walk and figure it out together."

1. When has someone taken the time to understand my behavior instead of judging me for it?
2. How does the Father respond to me when I fail?
3. What steps can I rehearse in my mind now so that I can forgive and provide grace to a child or teen when the occasion arises?

_____
_____
_____
_____
_____
_____
_____
_____
_____
_____
_____
_____
_____
_____
_____
_____
_____
_____
_____

Prayer

*Jesus, I am so grateful for Your grace towards me. I need your
help maintaining relationship and extending grace to others. Amen.*

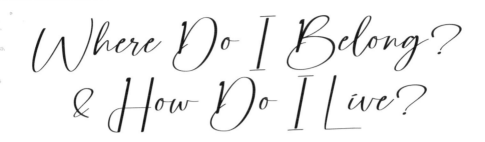

Where Do I Belong? & How Do I Live?

"Follow me, and I will make you fishers of men."
— MATTHEW 4:19 (ESV)

Jesus used these simple but powerful words to call His first disciples and in a single phrase, answered the two questions every human heart is asking:

Where do I belong?
How do I live?

Ryan had been asking these questions his whole life. Shuffled between family members before ending up in a group home at age seven, he had never known life without the ache of unmet needs.

For 15 years, he was one of "those kids" who had…
- no grandparent present at Grandparents' Day.
- no one showing up for parent teacher conferences.
- no family photos for show and tell.
- nobody saying, "You belong with me."

The school rules and group home guidelines told him how to live, but when you don't feel *wanted,* what's the point in doing what they say?

Then he met another kid just like him. Ryan and Vince became fast friends, and Vince introduced Ryan to other friends in the neighborhood. They offered Ryan protection, community, and a sense of belonging. And he would do anything to keep it.

- grab a few extra snacks in the checkout line
- take a little cash from the teacher's wallet
- steal the car parked on the corner
- anything to belong

Attachment is the answer to the question, "Where do I belong?" Jesus looked at each of his would-be-disciples and said, *"Follow me. You belong with me."*

Orientation answers the question, "How do I live?" Jesus told his first followers that they would fish for men. Along the journey, he would guide, correct, and shape their worldviews, and He will do the same for us, orienting us.

Attachment and orientation are *needs,* not desires or wants.[10] Because they are *needs,* if they aren't addressed in healthy ways, we will meet them, even if it's toxic.

Jesus looks at each of us and calls us to belong to Him, follow Him, and live like Him. Through Jesus Christ, we are given the right to become "children of God" (John 1:12), attached and grafted into God's family—our forever place to belong. And His Word orients us, teaching us how to live within His family. God outlined this plan way back in the days of the prophet Jeremiah, articulating how He would meet our two greatest needs.

> *For this is the covenant that I will make with the house of Israel after those days, declares the Lord: I will put my law within them, and I will write it on their hearts. And I will be their God, and they shall be my people.*
>
> — JEREMIAH 31:33 (ESV)

- With *"They shall be my people,"* He gives attachment—answering the question "Where do I belong?"
- With *"I will put my law within them,"* He gives orientation—answering the question "How should I live?"

Jesus extends the same invitation today to belong to Him and live like Him. Will we allow Him to meet our needs, or will we look to the world?

Trauma—informed Tip

The need for attachment and orientation drives behavior. When a child or teen does not have their need for attachment and orientation met through healthy relationships, they look elsewhere. Most often, unattached kids attach to other unattached kids.[11] As safe adults, we can actively cultivate connection, belonging, and attachment with children and teens from hard places. Try using a shared interest, such as working on a car, baking cookies, or playing a game together to bridge the gap between you and the child by engaging in a shared activity you both enjoy.

1. What are the places or groups where I seek belonging?
2. Where do I look for direction on how to live?
3. What is one practical activity I can invite someone to participate in this week?

_____

_____

_____

_____

_____

_____

_____

_____

_____

_____

_____

_____

_____

_____

_____

_____

_____

_____

_____

_____

Prayer

Lord, I belong to you! Thank you for the invitation to be in Your family.
Help me to see my identity as Your kid. Amen.

The Power of a Band-aid

Fear not, for I am with you; be not dismayed, for I am your God; I will strengthen you, I will help you, I will uphold you with my righteous right hand.

—ISAIAH 41:10 (ESV)

Sixteen-year-old KJ let out an expletive-filled outburst and proceeded to rip up the paper he was working on. It was a common occurrence at the after-school program where he spent his afternoons. "This is so stupid. Why do we even have to learn Algebra? I'll never use this in my life!"

Although KJ's behavior was not new, what *was* new was the reaction of his long-time tutor, Ms. Aniyah, who quietly approached KJ and pulled something from her pocket. "KJ, it looks like you're hurting. How about a band-aid?"

"Why would you ask me if I need a band-aid? Does it look like I'm bleeding?"

Kneeling down to look KJ in the eye, Ms. Aniyah explained, "I care about you KJ, and while I can't see everything that makes you hurt, offering a band-aid is my way of saying I'm here for you. I want to help."

After many more interactions like this—outburst, band-aid; outburst, band-aid; outburst, band-aid—KJ began to *ask* for a band-aid *before* he had an outburst. After several months, the outbursts stopped without a band-aid at all. Ms. Aniyah had slowly let KJ know he could ask for help from her whenever he needed, minimizing his frustration and giving him a needed and compassionate resource. KJ learned to seek out the care he needed *before* he had an outburst instead of picking up the pieces afterward.

At the end of the school year, and after passing Algebra, KJ approached Ms. Aniyah. "Thanks for making sure I understood math. I got you something." KJ handed Ms. Aniyah a new box of band-aids and said smiling, "I wanted to be sure you had enough for your students next year."

There are four key abilities necessary for "secure attachment:" [12]

- the ability to seek care
- the ability to give care
- the ability to feel comfortable with an autonomous self
- the ability to negotiate

Using her trauma-informed skills, Ms. Aniyah interrupted destructive patterns in KJ's life. Over time, this allowed KJ to *seek* care by asking for a band-aid. He *gave* care when he bought new band-aids for Ms. Aniyah to use with her new students. And, he *felt comfortable* being himself amongst the people around him. His attachment with others was improving.

Establishing secure, healthy attachment before asking anything of His followers is a hallmark of Jesus's ministry. We see an example of this in the story captured in John 21 of an encounter between Jesus and one of his disciples, Peter. In the years after this interaction, Peter would become one of the most influential figures in the early church, but at the time of this conversation, Peter had recently and publicly denied any association with Jesus.

"Peter, do you love me?" Jesus asks his friend three times. Through this gentle, repeated questioning, Jesus is carefully rebuilding the connection He and Peter once had and communicating *I care about you. I'm here for you. I want to help.* Only after their connection has been reestablished does Jesus then command Peter to "feed my sheep" and "follow me" (John 21:17, 19).

Jesus prioritizes relational connection. Secure attachment *with* Him is a prerequisite to working *for* Him.

Trauma—informed Tip

Even if skills for healthy relationships were not learned in early childhood, you can still intentionally teach them now. Have a box of band-aids on hand to give children the opportunity to both seek and receive care when they are hurting physically or emotionally. When you see a child use skills for healthy relationships such as asking for help, negotiating for what they need, or receiving a hug when offered, celebrate those moments by recognizing them as signs of healing.

1. Am I more apt to seek care or give care? Where did I learn this? Why is it important to be able to do both?
2. What are other examples of Jesus forming secure attachment with the people around Him?
3. How can I celebrate a child today who is using their skills to build healthy relationships?

_____

_____

_____

_____

_____

_____

_____

_____

_____

_____

_____

_____

_____

_____

_____

_____

_____

_____

_____

_____

Prayer

Jesus, I want to know Your love in new ways. Help me to be on the lookout for all the ways You express that love towards me. Amen.

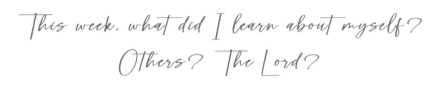

This week, what did I learn about myself?
Others? The Lord?

_____
_____
_____
_____
_____
_____
_____
_____
_____
_____
_____
_____
_____
_____
_____
_____
_____
_____
_____
_____
_____
_____
_____
_____
_____
_____
_____

I remember to think about the many things you did in years gone by. Then I lift my hands in prayer, because my soul is a desert, thirsty for water from you.

— PSALM 143:5–6 (CEV) —

Week 3

The Past Matters

God is present and active in every year, every day, and every moment of our lives. Our pasts hold stories of hurt and loss and stories of love and nourishment all woven together, shaping us. Only by first looking backward can we trace the hand of God in our lives, lift our hands in prayer, and find water for our thirsty souls.

This week we will turn around and remember where we have come from, learn how to process our experiences, release what we were not meant to carry, and walk into a life of freedom and flourishing.

How We See the World

For nothing will be impossible with God.

— LUKE 1: 37 (ESV)

A belief system is like a pair of glasses. It's the set of lenses we use to see the world around us. These lenses magnify, clarify, and often distort the way we see ourselves, others, and the world. Fine-tuned and continually adjusted since before we were even born, every person's individualized, customized pair of glasses is formed by two main ingredients: words and experiences.

At 13 years old, Amy already had her own set of belief system glasses. Growing up in a home full of conflict and chaos, words like "stupid", "in the way", and "a bad kid" had rained down, shaping and forming Amy's beliefs about herself. Words of anger and hate that her parents hurled at one another shaped her view of adults and relationships. Experiences of abuse and neglect by those who were supposed to care for her only confirmed that the negative words she had been collecting must be true. And, on top of it all, the experience of being bullied at school taught Amy the world was just as unsafe as her home. These are the glasses through which Amy saw the world. That is, until the day she met Sarah, her newly assigned mentor. Sarah knew how the power of words and experiences can shape a person, and she focused on giving Amy new ones.

As Sarah and Amy spent time together, Sarah spoke new words into Amy's belief system—words like, "You're so fun to be around," "You're a great kid," and "I believe in you." They spent time at the zoo, the park, having dinner, and laughing together. New words and experiences began to recalibrate the lenses Amy used to view herself, others, and the world around her.

Research shows that our brains are constantly growing, changing, and "rewiring" in response to words and experiences. This capacity is called *neuroplasticity* and it is good news for Amy and for us all. [13]

Paul is talking about neuroplasticity when he writes in Romans 12:2,

> *"Do not conform any longer to the pattern of this world,*
> *but be transformed by the renewing of your mind."*

Our beliefs impact the way we live our lives, but God designed our brains with the ability to change those beliefs. We can renew our minds with new words and experiences, and then behavior will follow. In Jesus' ministry, He was regularly depositing new and life-giving words and experiences into the lives of tax collectors, prostitutes, and sinners—people who had heard harmful words and had painful experiences. Mary Magdalene is one such example. In response to Jesus' kindness towards her, she became generous, was invitational, took risks, and her belief system calibrated with the gospel. Eventually, she was the first person to see the resurrection, and God trusted her to go and tell others (John 18).

Trauma-informed Tip

Every interaction with a child or teen from a hard place is an opportunity to deposit new words and experiences into their belief system. Think of one or two words and one new experience you can give them this week. It could be as simple as saying, "You're a great kid" or giving the experience of playing a game together.

1. What is one way that my belief system has been affected negatively through words or experiences?
2. In what way do those words or experiences change my view of God or myself?
3. Who can I intentionally provide new words or experiences for this week?

_____

Prayer

Jesus, I want to believe change is possible in me and in others.
Thank you for the work You do in us. Amen.

What We Weren't Meant To Carry

The Lord is near to the brokenhearted and saves the crushed in spirit.
— PSALM 34:18 (ESV)

Fifteen-year-old James was taking in a lot during the weekend. He kept to himself, but noticed everything around him—the lessons being taught, nightly conversations in the cabins, and what his peers were bravely sharing with each other. It was the first spiritual retreat he'd ever attended and all of it felt completely foreign to him.

James had spent the bulk of his life caring for himself and acting as the protector for his younger brothers. Growing up, he'd not attended church or really talked about God much. But now, his foster parents had signed him up for a youth retreat, and he was challenged to address the weight he'd carried for so long.

What was the "elephant in the room" of his life? What burden and hurt had he been shouldering alone? What was becoming a barrier between him and the life God had for him?

At the end of the night, a large, black, cut-out elephant took up a space where all the retreat-goers gathered outside. As the speaker finished up, he challenged the group to think deeply about what was holding them back. He invited the teens to approach the cut-out and write their "elephant" as a way of symbolically laying down their past.

James slowly approached. He knew exactly what his elephant was. All the emotions held at bay flooded to the surface as he wrote down the names of his brothers, releasing himself from the responsibility of being their caregiver. They were safe in a good foster home with adults who loved and provided for them. It was time to cultivate dreams for himself. As he stepped back to look at his handwriting on the cut-out, his pain, anger, despair, and discouragement were replaced with relief, hope, and joy. The next morning James was baptized, rising out lighter and understanding his past did not define his future.

James's story illustrates that if we don't give voice to the burdens we carry, we'll never experience true healing.

A psalm of praise, Psalm 147:3 says the Lord *"heals the brokenhearted and binds up their wounds."* It is not God's design for His children to walk burdened and broken.

1 Peter 2:24 points us to Jesus.

> *"He bore our sins in His body on the tree, that we might die to sin and live to righteousness. By His wounds you have been healed."*

Stop for a minute and breathe in this truth. *Really* let it sink in. Then take another deep breath and let it sink deeper. Repeat as needed. Jesus waits for us to unload our burdens on Him. He takes them—the things He never intended for us to carry and the shame of keeping them locked inside—and He carries them all the way to the cross.

We can help children acknowledge their past and the burdens they have picked up along the way by helping them understand the story of what happened to them. Be careful to take into consideration the child's age and maturity. Tell the story to them (if you know something they don't) with honesty and without judgment as many times as they need to hear it. Or if you are hearing it from them, actively and empathetically listen as they tell their perspective of it. Although it may seem repetitive, this helps a child make sense of their past and how that past impacts the present.

1. What might change for me if I experience freedom from my past?
2. What is my "elephant"? What is holding me back from what God has for me?
3. How can I better seek to understand the history of a child or teen? How do I remind myself (and them) that their past does not define their future plans?

_____

_____

_____

_____

_____

_____

_____

_____

_____

_____

_____

_____

_____

_____

_____

_____

_____

_____

_____

_____

_____

Prayer

*Lord, take my burdens! I don't want to carry them around anymore—
not in my mind, heart, or body. I give them to You. Relieve me. Amen.*

Don't Like It.
Can't Change It

Bri ran out of the classroom and into the sanctuary of the church where she attended school. She sat down abruptly in one of the pews. A teacher calmly sat on the other end and breathed deeply in the silence for about ten minutes. This wasn't Bri's first time fleeing from the classroom, and her teacher sensed that she felt out of control.

Bri's breathing slowed down in those ten minutes, but she still seemed agitated. She gestured wildly to the podium. "Why don't you go on stage and make a speech?" she asked the teacher.

Wisely, her teacher went along with it, walking slowly to the stage. She hoped the answer to her next question would give her insight into Bri. "What do you want to learn about?"

Bri sighed, "Who is Jesus? I've heard you talk about Him, but I don't understand."

Bri listened while the teacher shared some of Jesus's promises and allowed her to ask questions. Then Bri asked if it could be *her* turn on stage. Standing behind the podium, she could barely see over the wood, her words tumbling out in an order that only made sense to her.

"Thank you all for being here today… I am here to tell you about my mom. She is dead. I keep hoping I am in a dream, and I will wake up and she's here. But this is not a dream. She always said I got on her nerves, and now I can't say sorry. Tito told my sister and me she was dead and we're old enough to understand, but Micah is too young. He's not even going to remember her. *I want to remember her.* I miss her so much."

Bri rushed off stage and fell into the arms of the teacher who patiently held space for her grieving.

After some time, her crying slowed, and she calmly said, "I'm ready to go upstairs now." Nothing changed about Bri's situation, however she spent the rest of the day focused and willing to do her school work.

Like Bri, we all have parts of our story we don't like but can't change:[14]

- people we have lost
- tragedy we have experienced
- injustice we have suffered
- disappointment we never expected

There is always going to be a collision of what we want and hope for with what we don't like and can't change. It's more comfortable to feel mad than sad.

True healing is born out of *grief*—the acknowledgement of pain's presence. We need to feel the weight of loss, giving voice to how it impacts us. Crying, lamenting, and mourning are passageways to healing.

Ecclesiastes 3 reminds us, "*There is a time for everything, and a season for every activity under the heavens: a time to break down, and a time to build up; a time to weep, and a time to laugh; a time to mourn, and a time to dance.*"

If this is your time to feel the weightiness of your own grief or sadness, know that healing awaits. If you're helping someone else through this season, ask the Lord for His grace, patience, and wisdom. The road can feel long and painful, but on the other side of grief is acceptance. And that is where we find healing.

Trauma-informed Tip

The root of frustration and aggression in a child or teen with a traumatic past is often a mental collision with something they don't like and can't change—either in their current reality or past history. Safe adults can guide them through the grieving process by simply staying present, listening, and empathizing with the pain of loss—no fixing or advice needed. If a child begins to cry, allow them to cry, listening and remaining close.

1. What are some things in my life that I do not like and cannot change?
2. Have I been honest with God about the pain of these disappointments? How do I believe God would respond if I expressed my pain and sadness?
3. If I am not in my own season of grieving, what can I do to create space for a grieving friend?

_____

_____

_____

_____

_____

_____

_____

_____

_____

_____

_____

_____

_____

_____

_____

_____

_____

_____

_____

_____

_____

Prayer

*Jesus, there is so much to grieve. Help me to let go and share
with You what is hard and sad. Fill us with Your light. Amen.*

The Power of Feeling Heard

And He has given us this command: Anyone who loves God must also love their brother and sister.

— 1 JOHN 4:21

"**I**'m the common denominator in everything bad, I don't like any of this, and there is nothing I can do to change it," Calvin barely whispered through gritted teeth and angry tears.

Calvin had never told anyone the whole story—the way his mom and dad had fought for years or that no matter how hard he tried, he couldn't protect his sister from their neighbor. Then there was the nine months they lived in the women's shelter where the other kids would taunt, tease, and gang up on him, "the new kid." It was so bad that they finally sent Calvin and his siblings to the children's home. Their first day there, Calvin watched in agony as his siblings cried for him, terrified of the strangers walking them to their new rooms. They had never spent a night away from each other. All of this felt like his fault, and he was powerless to fix it.

After the story finally came out, he was shocked as he opened his eyes to see that John was still there. This new caregiver had seemed nice enough, but Calvin had never expected him to actually listen. *Weren't adults always too busy? Why wasn't he saying anything? Don't adults always have a sermon or correction ready?*

Instead, John listened, not trying to fix anything or make him feel better. And somehow, even though John said nothing at all, Calvin felt lighter.

We need to tell our stories.

A story holding a painful memory is a heavy burden to bear—one we weren't meant to carry alone. In fact, the brain often forms a "protective barrier" around a traumatic memory, blurring out the details but keeping all of the emotion bubbling under the surface. We may experience emotions that seem unconnected to any specific incident. Those emotions become manageable once they have a place to land, and the story is told.

Before children and teens will open a doorway to their painful past, there must be trust. They need to trust that someone will stay—not judge, lecture, or condemn them. They need to trust they are being heard.

In his letter to the Galatians, Paul instructs the new church to "*bear one another's burdens, and so fulfill the law of Christ*" (Galatians 6:2, ESV). By supporting one another, they would fulfill the call of Jesus to love one another.

It is tempting to confuse the role of burden bearer with burden fixer. It's hard to watch people we love feel the weight of pain and loss. The greatest gift we can give is our presence. It matters. When we try to fix the pain rather than be present in it, we cut off grief's necessary course and exhaust ourselves.

Trauma-informed Tip

It is a common misconception that there are experiences kids will be "too young to remember." Even trauma occurring before a person is born is remembered in the body.[16] Moreover, trauma experienced before a child acquires language skills is difficult to process later since they lack the ability to match the experience with words to describe it. When a child or teen shares a difficult experience from their past, do all you can to *stop everything else* and listen. If you are driving, turn down the music. If you're returning a quick email, save it for later. Turn your full attention to the child by letting them know with your eyes, body language, and calm presence that you are ready to listen. Dr. Dan Siegel teaches that when a person tells their story to an empathic listener, brain circuitry changes, and the brain begins to heal.[17]

1. When has someone listened to me without trying to fix anything? How did that feel?
2. What holds me back from coming to God so He can be a "listener" for me?
3. Do I need to tell my own story? Who would be a good listener? Am I willing to listen to someone else's story? How can I ensure I'm the best listener I can be?

_____

_____

_____

_____

_____

_____

_____

_____

_____

_____

_____

_____

_____

_____

_____

_____

_____

_____

_____

_____

Prayer

Lord, I want to be a better listener to You and to others.
Thank you for listening to me. Give me the heart to sit with others. Amen.

God's Kids

"To all who did receive him, to those who believed in his name,
he gave the right to become children of God."
— JOHN 1:12

Francisco's mom received the text from an unknown number. "Francisco forgot his soccer shoes. Can you bring them to school?"

Lucia's newly adopted son didn't have a cell phone, so she guessed a friend texted on his behalf. It was game day for his junior high soccer team. Lucia was quick to leave work and head home to investigate and sure enough, right by the door was Francisco's soccer bag—left in the rush of the morning. Grabbing them and heading to school, she found him in study hall.

"Forget something?" she asked, smiling. His face lit up. "It worked," he marveled. "I told my teammates I couldn't play because I didn't remember to bring my cleats. They told me *my mom* would bring them to school. I didn't know moms did that. But, look! You're here!" He forgot where he was for a moment and threw his arms around her.

Lucia whispered something in his ear about how moms do this kind of thing *all* the time. As she hugged him back, she realized Francisco's understanding of a healthy parent/child relationship was brand new. She was getting a chance to show him how it works. Having spent most of his childhood without a permanent home, Francisco still didn't understand all the rights that came with being someone's child.

Romans 8:15 underscores this gospel truth:

> *"The Spirit you received does not make you slaves, so that you live in fear again; rather, the Spirit you received brought about your adoption to sonship. And by him we cry, 'Abba, Father.'"*

For a variety of reasons, even as God's kids, we have rights we often don't fully appreciate or take advantage of. Our view of God as a "parent" is colored by our experiences with our earthly parents—both good and bad.

- Maybe your family was uncomfortable with big emotions, shutting down or minimizing them.
- Maybe your most important relationships in childhood were inconsistent—sometimes present and engaged and other times absent and preoccupied.
- Or maybe, even harder, those closest to you were erratic and abusive. The ones you were supposed to trust and run to for safety were also your source of terror.

We take the patterns we learned as kids and follow them like well-worn paths, expecting each relationship we engage in to lead to the same place. This continues until we take the courageous step to follow a new path—the most important path—of God becoming our Father and us learning how to be His kid.

The good news is we are no longer slaves to any of the patterns we once learned in childhood!

God is the *perfect* parent. When He adopts us into His family and calls us His own, He teaches us a new pattern for relationships. He can handle our big emotions. He will never abandon us. He will never abuse or harm us. He works all things for our good.

Trauma-informed Tip

We often parent or interact with children in the way we were parented. For some, that instinct brings healthy patterns. For others, the patterns are destructive. For all of us, the patterns are imperfect. By reflecting on your own experiences as a child, you grow in understanding.

- What patterns were modeled by your parents?
- How was discipline handled in your home?
- What happened when you were hurt and needed comfort?

Once you have reflected on and identified learned patterns, you can intentionally choose how to engage with the children in your life. For example, if your parents did not offer hugs as a form of care when you were hurt, look for opportunities to offer comfort through a hug. If forgiveness was modeled well, double-down with the children around you in a similar way.

1. What patterns were modeled by my parents? How did those patterns make me feel? How do I tend to mimic those as I have grown?
2. How has my view of God been shaped by my view of my parents? What characteristics have I assigned to God? (Remember, these characteristics could be a true or untrue reflection of God.)
3. How can I show a child what a gracious and merciful God is really like this week? Can I be more generous? Can I sacrifice my time? Can I listen without speaking?

_____

_____

_____

_____

_____

_____

_____

_____

_____

_____

_____

_____

_____

_____

_____

_____

_____

_____

_____

Prayer

Jesus, I am so grateful to be Your kid. Thank you for bringing me into Your family.
May I reflect daily what that means to those around me. Amen.

This week, what did I learn about myself? Others? The Lord?

The Lord is my shepherd; I shall not want.

— **PSALM 23:1 (ESV)** —

What We Need Matters

With the Lord as our Shepherd, we always have what we need; we "shall not want."

He's the ultimate Provider—of manna in the desert, water in the wilderness, and rest for weary souls.

He's our Protector, Defender, Comforter, and faithful Friend.

He provides food for the ravens, clothes fields in wildflowers, and puts food on tables.

He sees our needs before we even know to ask, and we can trust Him.

This week we will look at some of the deepest needs in each of our lives. We will see the ways God has already provided, look for what is motivating behavior, and learn that meeting needs is a doorway to deeper and truer connection with God and others.

We Need Care in Every Area

I am the LORD your God, who brought you up out of the land of Egypt.
Open your mouth wide, and I will fill it.
— PSALM 81:10 (ESV)

"I'm going to quit," Jemar stated matter-of-factly. Laura couldn't believe what she was hearing. Two weeks into college, Jemar was already giving up.

Frustrated and disappointed, she replayed the list of all she had given him since he came into their family three years ago. He had a roof over his head, food to eat, new clothes, new shoes, new backpack, new computer, and the list could go on forever.

Laura began mentally calculating all the money spent and all the things she had sacrificed so he could have what he needed—including a private tutor and ACT prep classes—all in an effort to get him into college. Now he wanted to just quit?

It didn't make any sense. Didn't he have everything he needed?

Laura isn't alone. Her frustration with Jemar is an all-too-common story.

Our eyes are drawn to the worn out tennis shoes, broken backpack, lack of medical care, and empty kitchen cupboards. These are easy entry points to make a difference. However, physical needs are only one part of the equation.

Jemar did have every *thing* he needed, but he didn't have the social and emotional skills to navigate a college experience. He didn't know how to talk to professors and ask for extra help when he needed it. He didn't know how to make and maintain friendships with his peers and navigate the complex social structure of dorm life.

Jemar needed *holistic* care that recognized the interconnectedness of each area of his development—spiritual, physical, educational, emotional, and social. Laura could choose to be frustrated with Jemar and use incentives or manipulation to get him back in school. Or, she could do the work of listening to Jemar to understand where their plans to prepare him for this next stage needed more development. The latter might feel like more work initially, but it will create a path of healing that gives Jemar the best chance for growth and success.

God recognizes the interconnectedness of our beings. He knitted us together, after all. So, it makes sense God's provision in *our* lives extends to all areas of our development.

Before sin entered the world and interrupted the perfect nature of God's creation, Adam and Eve's needs were met in every area.

- Spiritually - In direct relationship with God, Adam and Eve enjoyed their intimate and daily connection with Him.
- Physically - God provided a safe place to live, fruit to eat, and rivers of water to drink.
- Educationally - Adam and Eve were continually learning—what plants to eat, the animals to name, the way to live.
- Emotionally - There was joy, fulfilment, and only healthy and life-giving responses to any challenge.
- Socially - Adam and Eve were completely satisfied by their companionship with one another.

God's provision for Adam and Eve models the path of holistic care we would be wise to follow. Thank you, Lord, for tending to our every need!

Trauma-informed Tip

When working with children or teens who have experienced trauma, try creating a holistic care plan. This plan should include a growth goal in each of the five areas of development and some specific steps to achieve those goals. Be careful to tailor the plan to meet the current developmental level and individual needs of each child.

1. Thinking back to childhood, what is one way each of the five main areas of development were met in my life?
2. Where in Scripture do I see Jesus tending to one (or more) of the five areas of development in someone He is interacting with?
3. Who is someone in my life not receiving care in one of the five areas of need? What is a practical way I can show the love of Christ by meeting that need this week?

_____

_____

_____

_____

_____

_____

_____

_____

_____

_____

_____

_____

_____

_____

_____

_____

_____

_____

_____

*Jesus, there is nothing unseen to You. Thank you for caring
for my whole self and for tending to my every need. Amen.*

We Need To Feel Safe

You who fear the Lord, trust in the Lord. He is their help and their shield!
— PSALM 115:11 (ESV)

Whether we realize it or not, we all have three questions playing on a loop inside our heads:

Am I safe?

If the answer is yes, then we ask…

Am I loved?

If the answer is yes, then—and only then—will we ask…

What can I learn?

For years, teachers shook their heads and nearly gave up on 13-year-old Erica. No matter how many extra assignments she was given or special tutoring sessions she attended, nothing clicked. What nobody took into account was the reality of the group home Erica had been living in for the last ten years, with its revolving list of caregivers and kids who bullied her for her weight. Everyone was frustrated Erica "couldn't learn", but they had failed to answer the first two questions her brain was constantly asking.

Even though she was physically secure, did Erica *feel* safe?
Even though there were adults who cared, did Erica *feel* loved?

The answer became clear once she moved into a foster home with Dan and Julie. On her first day, the couple greeted her at the door and gave her a tour of her new home. After years of sharing everything, she couldn't believe they made space just for her. Each day followed the same pattern: school, homework, time to relax, and family dinner. Erica experienced consistency for the first time. Erica not only *was* safe, but she also *felt* safe.

Each night, Dan and Julie would repeat the same words as Erica headed to bed. "You are incredible. You are important. And it makes us so happy to have you here." She thought it was weird at first, but after a while it became her favorite part of their evening routine. Erica began to not only *believe* she was loved, but she also *felt* loved.

Dan and Julie answered the questions her brain was asking: *Do I feel safe? Do I feel loved?* The resounding yes she received to those two questions led to her bursting through the front door waving her report card.

"I got an A- in science!" she squealed. Erica's brain finally felt safe and loved enough to ask, *What can I learn?*

If "felt safety" isn't present or children question whether they're loved, accomplishing daily tasks and learning new skills can be challenging. Felt safety, as defined by the late Dr. Karyn Purvis, is "when you arrange the environment and adjust your behavior so your children can feel in a profound and basic way that they are truly safe in their home with you. Until your child experiences safety for himself or herself, trust can't develop, and healing and learning won't progress." [18]

When adults create an environment with felt safety, they invite children into a space of healing *and* learning.

In the accounts of the births of both John the Baptist and Jesus, God established the feeling of safety in what, undoubtedly, felt like a frightening series of events. Is it any surprise the angels delivering His message began their interactions with, "Do not be afraid"?

When Zechariah needed to understand that his wife was having a child, the angel said to him,

"Do not be afraid, Zechariah; your prayer has been heard. [You are safe and can now truly hear what I have to proclaim!] Your wife Elizabeth will bear you a son, and you are to call him John."

— LUKE 1:13

Mary, when visited by an angel, was told,

"Do not be afraid, Mary; you have found favor with God. [You are safe and can now truly hear what I have to proclaim!] You will conceive and give birth to a son, and you are to call him Jesus."

— LUKE 1:30–31

On the night of Jesus' birth, the shepherds were terrified by the light of the glory of the Lord shining all around them. Yet again an angel says,

"Do not be afraid! I bring you good news that will cause great joy for all the people. [You are safe and can now truly hear what I have to proclaim!] Today in the town of David a Savior has been born to you; he is the Messiah, the Lord. This will be a sign to you: You will find a baby wrapped in cloths and lying in a manger."

— LUKE 2:10–12

God communicated in such a way that each of these important people in His unfolding story would feel "in a profound and basic way" that they were "truly safe." Doing so allowed each to learn of the good news and their specific role in the arrival of the Savior.

God longs for us—important players in His unfolding story—to know we are safe and loved. His desire is for us to "profoundly experience" the safety and love He provides.

Trauma-informed Tip

Children and teens who have experienced early trauma will only truly thrive in an environment where they *feel* safe.[19] There is a big difference in being physically safe and actually *feeling* safe. Next time you engage with a child or teen who is struggling to learn, ask yourself, *Do they feel safe? Do they feel loved?* If not, stop and address these two questions before continuing with the lesson. For example, help a child feel safe by lowering your body posture at or below eye level, checking your tone of voice, and meeting any physical needs like thirst or hunger. Help a child feel loved with gentle eye contact, encouraging words, and a playful attitude. Be considerate of children with learning disabilities or those who suffer from the long-lasting impact of trauma on the brain. Seek to understand their potential and work toward creating a healthy and safe place for them to grow.

Children and teens with a history of physical or sexual abuse have experienced a violation of their personal space and an inappropriate form of touch. Be careful to avoid suddenly approaching a child or teen from behind. It is highly likely any form of unanticipated touch could trigger a fear response. Increase felt safety by using "safe-touch". Ask permission before entering a child or teen's personal space. Ask, "Can I have a hug?" or "Can I get a high-five?"

1. What makes a person or place feel safe to me?
2. How has God communicated to me that *I am safe* and *I am loved?*
3. Who can I help feel safe and loved? Have I ever asked what I can do to make them feel that way?

_____

_____

_____

_____

_____

_____

_____

_____

_____

_____

_____

_____

_____

_____

_____

_____

_____

_____

_____

_____

_____

Prayer

Jesus, wherever I am, with You, I am safe. Thank you for always being with me. You are my strength and my shield. Amen.

We Need To be Understood

I the Lord search the heart and test the mind, to give every man according to his ways, according to the fruit of his deeds.

— JEREMIAH 17:10 (ESV)

"**N**O! I won't shower, and you can't make me," Andrew shouted at his foster mom Sarah, triggering her own wave of anger and defensiveness. Threats were made, voices raised, and doors slammed. She ultimately won, but at what cost? With Andrew finally showered and in bed, Sarah collapsed, exhausted and confused. This angry, defiant child was not Andrew. Most days he was pleasant, kind, teachable, and a joy to be around. This newfound attitude felt personal and insurmountable.

The battle raged on for days. Everything Sarah asked of him was met with resistance. Every time she tried to connect, he pushed her further away. Confused, frustrated, and out of options, she finally began to ask, "Why?"

Why was he acting this way?
Why had his behavior changed so drastically?
Was there a specific event that set this battle into motion?

As she traced the timeline and "chased the why," she made a phone call to Andrew's biological aunt, whom he had visited just a few weeks before. Sarah asked a few questions about their time together. After a few minutes of small talk, Andrew's aunt mentioned that her brother would be released from jail next month and would likely move in with her. Alarm bells began to sound in Sarah's head as pieces of the puzzle slid into place. This aunt's brother is Andrew's father—the same man who physically abused Andrew and his siblings and sold his younger sister into sex trafficking. He was about to walk right back into Andrew's world.

Taking a deep breath, Sarah asked quietly, "Does Andrew know?"

"I think we talked about it, yes, but he seemed just fine with it. . ." came the aunt's quick response.

Suddenly the meaning behind Andrew's behavior became clear. Feeling scared and vulnerable, *of course* he was grasping for control anywhere he could find it. *Of course* he was pushing her away. Now that she knew the "why," she could ask the next question: *What does he need?*

Sarah spent weeks fighting Andrew's behavior until she realized that, like the tip of an iceberg, what she was seeing was only what's above the surface. The same is true in every relationship. There is almost always more going on below the surface. And when we only fight what we can see, we miss the need behind that behavior.

I Samuel 16:7 says,

> *"Man looks at the outward appearance, but the Lord looks at the heart."*

This is what Jesus did with the Pharisees. He rebuked them because they became too focused on outward appearances—on the tip of the iceberg above the surface. In Matthew 23, He calls them "whitewashed tombs" and "hypocrites", calling attention to the ways they "wash the outside of the cup", but leaving the inside full of greed and selfishness.

Jesus is more concerned with the condition of hearts and the meaning behind behavior than He is with the behavior itself. He longs to meet the deepest needs of our hearts, not force us to comply with a set of behavioral expectations. Jesus relentlessly "chases the why." He invites us to look under the surface, find the underlying need, and allow Him to meet it. We look like Him when we don't settle for only what we can see, but instead relentlessly look for the meaning behind the behavior.

Trauma-informed Tip

When faced with challenging behavior from a child or teen who has a history of trauma, take a deep breath and ask yourself, "What is the meaning behind this behavior?" Is there a physical need? Is the child hungry, angry, lonely, or tired? Has there been a relational shift or loss? Are there changes in the environment causing fear and anxiety of the unknown? Become a detective, assess all sides of the situation, and ask, "What need are they trying to meet when they behave this way?" Once you find the need, commit yourself to meeting it.

---

1. When has an unmet need (e.g., hunger, loneliness, or weariness) impacted the way I behaved?
2. What can I do to become—like God—a "detective" of my own heart and the hearts of people around me?
3. What are one or two action steps I can take to ensure I don't merely react, but instead slow down and seek to understand *why* a child or teen is misbehaving?

Prayer

God, thank You for seeing into me and knowing my heart and intention.
Forgive me where I am selfish and give me confidence where I am insecure. Amen.

Need Felt. Need Met.
Trust Built.

Every moving thing that lives shall be food for you.
And as I gave you the green plants, I give you everything.
— GENESIS 9:3 (ESV)

"I need a pencil."
"I need a sandwich."
"I need to take playdough to school."
"I need new shoes."
"I need my soccer uniform washed."
"I need a new phone."
"I need…"
"I need…"
"I need…"

It's all Louisa hears during the day—a clamor of needs coming from the mouths of the six children in her care. Some days it feels unending and overwhelming. But when she is able to shift her perspective and remember just two months ago when Nathan would wander into the kitchen and make his own sandwich, Kevin would wash his soccer uniform in the sink, and Chris would ask the other kids at school for pencils, she can see the progress they all have made together.

When they first arrived, no one asked her for anything. They didn't believe she would provide or could be trusted.

Now, every time they have a need, Louisa sees it as an opportunity. With her

renewed perspective, the unending, individual voices of need actually sound more like a chorus of trust.

Attachment is the connection between a child and their primary caregiver.[20] It is a critical bond formed through a repetitive cycle of experienced needs becoming *met* needs.

Imagine a newborn baby. What can a baby do to meet their own needs? Nothing. They can't fix their own bottle or grab a blanket when they are cold. The only thing they can do is cry, telling the world, "I need something," and hoping someone responds. This is the beginning of the attachment cycle and in an ideal world, a loving adult shows up to meet the need. The adult heats the bottle or grabs the blanket and the child calms down. A need is felt … A need is met … Trust is formed.

Exodus 16 gives us a clear picture of God as the One who meets our needs—the One who can be trusted.

> In the desert the whole community grumbled against Moses and Aaron. The Israelites said to them, "If only we had died by the Lord's hand in Egypt! There we sat around pots of meat and ate all the food we wanted, but you have brought us out into this desert to starve this entire assembly to death." Then the Lord said to Moses, "I will rain down bread from heaven for you. The Lord said to Moses, "I have heard the grumbling of the Israelites. Tell them, 'At twilight you will eat meat, and in the morning you will be filled with bread. Then you will know that I am the Lord your God.'" That evening quail came and covered the camp, and in the morning there was a layer of dew around the camp. When the dew was gone, thin flakes like frost on the ground appeared on the desert floor. When the Israelites saw it, they said to each other, "What is it?" For they did not know what it was. Moses said to them, "It is the bread the Lord has given you to eat."
>
> — EXODUS 16:2–4 ,11–15

God even provided water from a rock to quench the thirst of His people (Exodus 17:1–7).

God was the ultimate meeter of His people's needs. Every evening and morning, God met the needs of the nation of Israel, and, eventually, the people learned to trust Him. God heard the need. God met that need. His children learned to trust Him.

Centuries later, when asked by His disciples how to pray, Jesus includes a petition for "our daily bread." Jesus is reminding them of the story they had been told since childhood, reinforcing that God is the same kind of need-meeter He was for their people in Exodus.

God uses this same attachment cycle of "need felt, need met, trust built" to increase our attachment to Him. He wants to be our Source for everything we need. He wants to hear our needs and meet our needs, so we learn to trust Him more.

Trauma-informed Tip

Shift your perspective! Rather than viewing a request or expression of a need as another item on your to-do list, try viewing it as an opportunity to build trust. Trust is the solid foundation formed through attachment that opens up the door for greater connection, openness to direction, and heart-change in the life of a child or teen.

1. How have I seen God meet my needs?
2. Do I trust God to meet my needs? How do I know?
3. Who in my life lacks trust with me? What do they need from me to build this bridge of trust?

_____

_____

_____

_____

_____

_____

_____

_____

_____

_____

_____

_____

_____

_____

_____

_____

_____

Prayer

Lord, thank you for listening to my every need. I trust You in how and when You answer. I give You all the glory and rest in Your provision. Amen.

We Need Regulation: Moving from Dependence To Independence

And the peace of God, which surpasses all understanding,
will guard your hearts and your minds in Christ Jesus.
— PHILIPPIANS 4:7

They called him the "tiny tornado." At just six years old, Alex was already known for the way he could tear a room apart in a matter of seconds. It seemed any emotion—excitement, nervousness, anger—would inevitably spin him out of control and into destruction.

"Calm down."
"Get your act together."
"Act your age."

Magic words, threatened punishments, and well-meaning behavior management plans didn't make a difference. Out of options, adults typically left him alone until the storm subsided.

One day a new teacher arrived at Alex's school. Irwin took one look at this tiny tornado and rather than asking, "What is wrong with you?", he began to ask, "What happened to you?" or "What *didn't* happen that should have?"

Irwin provided snacks, water, and exercise, giving Alex the best chance at avoiding an outburst. When the tiny tornado began to spin, rather than send him away, Irwin remained close. He put his arm around Alex's shoulders and said, "Breathe deep with me. We'll count together—in 1, 2, 3, out 1, 2, 3." Slowly, the storm subsided.

Over time, Irwin taught Alex different and playful ways he could calm himself down. With new skills to use when his feelings surfaced, the "tiny tornado" no longer lived up to his nickname.

As infants, adults control our environment.: when we eat, when we sleep, and even how we calm down when we're feeling overwhelmed or afraid. The management of the world in this way is called *external regulation*. Someone outside of ourselves "regulates" our environment and how we react to it.

But sometime around two years old, we test a newfound free will. If we have trustworthy caregivers, we learn that the people around us will respond to our needs. We cry, and they give us a drink of water. We hold up our arms when we need a hug or want to feel safe, and we get picked up. The caregivers in our life hear our voice and work together with us in a process called *co-regulation.*

Ultimately, we learn to calm ourselves, by ourselves, in response to the world around us. This is called *self-regulation.*[21]

It's a skill most of us use successfully every day. When we're cut off in traffic, instead of yelling at the person who cut us off, we breathe deep, take a sip of water, or turn on the radio, and the moment passes.

We're not born knowing how to do this. It's a learned skill. External regulation leads to co-regulation which leads to self-regulation. Each stage is essential and can't be skipped.

If a stage is skipped, like in Alex's case, someone has to help us learn it—no matter how old we are. If no one does, we live in a state called *dysregulation.* In that state, our emotions lead us to behave in destructive and harmful ways to ourselves and the people and places around us.

It is comforting to know our God never abandons us in any stage of our life and is a consistent, loving presence walking with us through external, co-, and self-regulation.

God is constantly externally regulating our worlds; we are fully dependent on Him for everything. He is the consistent, single source of provision for every good thing in our lives. *"Every good and perfect gift is from above, coming down from the Father of the heavenly lights, who does not change like shifting shadows"* (James 1:17).

God also engages in co-regulation with us. We often are like a strong-willed two-year-old, desperate to display our independence while still being deeply dependent on someone else to help us manage the world around us.

When Jesus was arrested in the Garden of Gethsemane, Peter had some overwhelming emotions. He had just seen his friend betray Jesus, and the situation was increasingly feeling out of his control. In response, he pulled out his sword and cut off the ear of the slave of the high priest. He was fully dysregulated!

In Matthew 26:52–54 we see how Jesus co-regulates Peter by calmly speaking what was true. *"Put your sword back into its place; for all those who take up the sword will perish by the sword. Or do you think that I cannot appeal to My Father, and He will at once put at My disposal more than twelve legions of angels? How then would the Scriptures be fulfilled, which say that it must happen this way?"*

Jesus will often use truth to settle the lies threatening our peace. He tells us throughout Scripture to "set our minds on things above" (Colossians 3:2) and "take every thought captive" (2 Corinthians 10:5), knowing that when our minds are at peace, our actions will follow.

As we grow in co-regulation with God, self-regulation emerges as we exercise the Fruit of the Spirit—the power of God that resides with us (Galatians 5:22–23). Utilizing the presence of the Spirit, we are able to confidently interact with the world around us, regulating our emotions and actions and making choices in line with God's good will for our lives.

Trauma–informed Tip

Many children who experience early childhood trauma did not have an attuned and supportive caregiver walking them through the stages of external and co-regulation. Therefore, they never developed the skills necessary to self-regulate. When adults say "calm down" to a child who has lived this experience, it doesn't work. They do not know *how* to calm down. Instead, try engaging a child or teen in co-regulation. Work together to emotionally regulate through deep breathing, taking a walk, or talking it out. During quiet moments together, proactively teach calm-down strategies such as deep breathing or wall pushups that you can use together in moments of dysregulation.

1. In what ways have I seen God provide me with good and perfect gifts (i.e., external regulation)?
2. What are some things that "push my buttons" (i.e., dysregulate me)?
3. How do I calm myself down (i.e., self-regulate)? Are these strategies that might work with others as I co-regulate with them? Why or why not?

_____

_____

_____

_____

_____

_____

_____

_____

_____

_____

_____

_____

_____

_____

_____

_____

_____

_____

_____

Prayer

Lord, I can lose my cool and forget all You've done for me. Help me remember to take a minute to breathe and appreciate Your goodness and grace towards me. Amen.

This week, what did I learn about myself? Others? The Lord?

God is our safe place and our strength.
He is always our help when we are in trouble.

— PSALM 46:1 (NLV) —

Feeling Safe Matters

God offers Himself as our safe place, refuge, fortress, and strong tower because He knows *feeling* safe radically changes our experience. We have an enemy that wants us to live scared. He seeks to terrorize and destabilize because he knows when we feel safe we are able to connect deeply with others and with God. Our enemy wants nothing more than to use fear to trick us into living disconnected and disintegrated lives, but the good news is God moves into fear and chaos bringing peace, order, and connection.

This week we will look at how God increases our feeling of safety. We'll see the ways He meets us in the darkness, transforming our environment with His presence, provision, and predictability.

Light in the Darkness

But if we walk in the light, as he is in the light, we have fellowship with one another, and the blood of Jesus his Son cleanses us from all sin.

— 1 JOHN 1:7 (ESV)

They had watched his favorite movie, brushed his teeth with his special Superman toothbrush, and his favorite blankets were clean and waiting on his bed. Lauren had prepared everything for a smooth bedtime routine. In spite of all this, forty-five minutes later, six-year-old Jeffrey was still not asleep. Instead, he was bouncing in the bed, laughing hysterically, and humming a circus tune. Lauren felt like she was in the middle of a circus; this was *chaos*.

"Everybody is asleep, even the dog is asleep. Can't you go to sleep, too?" she pleaded. "Even the house is asleep! It's all dark!"

In that moment she remembered what was missing. She had noticed yesterday that Jeffrey's Superman night light was burned out, no longer casting the gentle glow around the bedroom. It was too dark. Jeffrey didn't feel safe.

Nothing about their routine had changed. Nothing about the actual level of safety in their home had changed. Jeffrey was as physically safe tonight as he had been every other night he had lived with them. However, without the Superman night light, Jeffrey's experience had changed. He no longer *felt* safe.

Lauren ran to the garage and grabbed a flashlight. "I know it's dark in here. Hold onto this flashlight and you can light up the room anytime you want." One more big bounce and Jeffrey was tucked under the covers, flashlight in hand and ready to sleep.

The darkness can feel scary. It's disorienting and unsettling, even when we know we are physically safe. A small change to Jeffrey's environment—the simple presence of a flashlight—increased his sense of felt safety and allowed him to rest.

The gospel of John says Jesus Christ is

"the true light that gives life to everyone"
— JOHN 1:9

His presence changes our environment and in His presence we can feel safe. As the Psalmist says,

"Even though I walk through the darkest valley, I will fear no evil"
— *Psalm 23:4*

His presence changes our experience in the same way the flashlight changed Jeffrey's experience in the darkness. We move from the reality of *being* safe to also *feeling* safe.

For children and teens who have experienced years of chronic unpredictability and unmet needs, the darkness can linger long after they have left the danger. They may be in a safe place, but they don't necessarily feel safe. As we are called to be imitators of Christ, we can offer our presence and whatever we have within our reach to help others feel safe in the midst of their own darkness.

Rejoice not over me, O my enemy; when I fall, I shall rise;
when I sit in darkness, the Lord will be a light to me.
— MICAH 7:8 (ESV)

God is not afraid of the darkness; He consistently moves toward it, changes it with His presence, and increases our sense of safety in the process. We look like Him when we do the same.

Trauma-informed Tip

Children and teens with a trauma history undoubtedly have experienced chaos and unpredictability. It's important, whenever possible, to maintain a consistent and predictable routine. Doing so helps them know what to expect, increasing their feeling of safety.

1. What's an example of a time my surroundings were safe, but I didn't *feel* safe? With that in mind, what are some important factors that make me *feel* safe?
2. Where have I seen God be the light in dark places?
3. How can I change the environment where I typically spend time with children or teens to make them feel more safe? Does the entire setting need to change or only pieces?

_____

_____

_____

_____

_____

_____

_____

_____

_____

_____

_____

_____

_____

_____

_____

_____

_____

_____

_____

_____

_____

_____

Prayer

Jesus, help me to see You wherever I am. I want to look at others and see them as You do. Teach me to live in Your light. Amen.

Something To Drink

I will pour water on the thirsty land, and streams on the dry ground.
— ISAIAH 44:3

"Hey, Amos. It's great to see you! Grab a water, a snack, and a book!"

This was the welcome Amos now heard every time he arrived at the summer reading program. With his apple slices, water bottle, and copy of *The Rainbow Fish* tucked under his arm, he made his way across the room to his tutor, D'Angelo.

The other tutors couldn't help but notice how different this entrance was from the one just two weeks earlier. The first day of the reading program, Amos ran laps in the parking lot instead of running to his tutor. Rather than calmly choosing a book to read, he dumped all the books onto the floor. He was unfocused, uncontrolled, and unable to read even one book that day.

After his first day, the staff team regrouped to figure out what they had missed. They had the books grouped by level, tutors ready and waiting, and posters of the rules around the room. What more could they need?

Finally a voice chimed in, "Do you think he was thirsty?"

Could it have been that simple? Did he just need water? The team decided to try it, and the results were astonishing. Amos, along with all the other children in the program, were calmer, more focused, less aggressive.

Water was the answer.

Water makes up 70% of the human body and 85% of an adult brain. It covers 75%

of the Earth's surface and is mentioned 722 times in the Bible. Water is essential to life; it's essential for growth, flourishing, and wellness.

When we experience thirst, our fear response automatically kicks in, knowing if we don't get something to drink, we won't survive. When the need is met, we feel safe.

As God spoke the world into existence, water came first because it was essential for everything else.

> *Now the earth was formless and empty, darkness was over the surface of the deep, and the Spirit of God was hovering over the waters.*
>
> — GENESIS 1:2

Our body doesn't just need water to survive. It needs water to function as it was designed. When we are dehydrated:

- We are more likely to be irritable.
- We are more likely to be violent.
- Our cognitive function slows down.
- We experience fatigue and exhaustion.

Is it any wonder Jesus chooses this as His primary illustration when revealing Himself to a Samaritan woman in the midday heat?

When a Samaritan woman came to draw water, Jesus said to her, "Will you give me a drink?" (His disciples had gone into the town to buy food.) The Samaritan woman said to him, "You are a Jew and I am a Samaritan woman. How can you ask me for a drink?" (For Jews do not associate with Samaritans.) Jesus answered her, "If you knew the gift of God and who it is that asks you for a drink, you would have asked him and he would have given you living water." "Sir," the woman said, "you have nothing to draw with and the well is deep. Where can you get this living water? Are you greater than our father Jacob, who gave us the well and drank from it himself, as did also his sons and his livestock?" Jesus answered, "Everyone who drinks this water will be thirsty again, but whoever drinks the water I give them will never thirst. Indeed, the water I give them will become in them a spring of water welling up to eternal life."

— JOHN 4:7–14

Trauma-informed Tip

A dehydrated child or teen may be more aggressive verbally and physically. Dehydration increases the neurotransmitter glutamate, which is associated with aggression.[22] Decrease violent outbursts and increase cognitive function by encouraging children and teens to drink water *at least every two hours.* Try giving each child a personal water bottle to keep with them throughout the day. Also, model healthy hydration by drinking water yourself!

1. Jesus calls himself the "living water"—a well that never ends. How have I seen His nourishment and refreshment in my life?
2. What areas of my life are "running dry" and need Jesus' living water?
3. How can I incorporate water—both physical and spiritual—into the time I spend with children and teens?

Jesus, You are the living water! Thank you for never running dry. I do not want to go to my own cisterns, but instead trust in Your unending supply. Amen.

Hangry

Listen, listen to me, and eat what is good, and you will delight in the richest of fare.

— ISAIAH 55:2

han·gry /'haNGgrē: bad-tempered or irritable as a result of hunger

Haven't we all been there? Snapping at people around us, losing the will to persevere through a challenge, frustrated over the slightest inconvenience... We blame the people, the challenge, and the inconvenience when a simple solution is available.

Antonio was twelve years old and had already walked a difficult road of traumatic experiences in a variety of housing situations. Hunger and malnourishment marked his early years, resulting in heightened levels of fear around feelings of hunger. Each time he felt hungry, his brain kicked into a protective state, ready to fight for what he needed and never forgetting the years when he didn't get it.

One afternoon, after a teacher requested he take out his notebook, he responded disrespectfully with angry grumbling and a few tipped chairs. Surveying the room's destruction, this trauma-informed teacher looked into his eyes and dug beneath the behavior to understand what he needed. Rather than engage in combat, she offered a peanut butter and jelly sandwich. Disarmed and confused, he accepted. Two bites later, he took his notebook out of his backpack and began his homework.

God had a similar experience with the prophet Elijah. Fleeing for his life, Elijah was all alone on his journey to Horeb. He found a broom bush, likely the only source of shade in the hot desert, and curled up under it, telling God he'd had enough and begging God to take his life. Exhausted, he fell asleep. Rather than responding to

Elijah's outburst, God met his underlying need; Elijah was hungry and dehydrated.

All at once an angel touched him and said, 'Get up and eat.' He looked around, and there by his head was some bread baked over hot coals, and a jar of water. He ate and drank and then lay down again. The angel of the Lord came back a second time and touched him and said, "Get up and eat, for the journey is too much for you." So he got up and ate and drank. Strengthened by that food, he traveled forty days and forty nights until he reached Horeb, the mountain of God.

— 1 KINGS 19:5–8

Once his need for food was met, Elijah was strengthened. God empowered Elijah with food so he could do what God was asking of him.

Hunger can hijack our emotions and behaviors like it did for Antonio and Elijah. Our bodies need consistent and healthy nourishment to function at their best, especially after traumatic experiences of extreme hunger or when a large amount of energy has been spent responding to abuse, neglect, and abandonment. It takes a lot of energy to be afraid.

Is there such a thing as being spiritually hangry? If the Word is the Bread of Life and we don't nourish our soul consistently, we may act out in the same way we do when physically hangry—snapping at people, giving up when things feel hard, and not feeling empowered to do what God is asking of us.

To empower is to equip—giving the body, brain, and spirit what it needs. When our basic physical needs are met, we feel safe. Our brain and body can relax, no longer worried it won't have what it needs to survive. Often this means looking beyond behavior to their underlying needs. And remember to exercise self-awareness to notice when you might be getting physically or spiritually hungry too.

Trauma-informed Tip

Prenatal exposure to alcohol or prolonged periods of hunger in early childhood alter the physical shape of insulin receptors.[23] These changes mean the brain often misinterprets messages of hunger as threats to safety, sending the brain into a fight, flight, or freeze response. To preemptively address hunger, provide food or healthy snacks every two hours. [15]

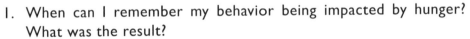

1. When can I remember my behavior being impacted by hunger? What was the result?
2. Why is my physical well-being important to God?
3. How can I incorporate healthy nutrition into my interactions with others, especially others who have experienced trauma?

_____

_____

_____

_____

_____

_____

_____

_____

_____

_____

_____

_____

_____

_____

_____

_____

_____

_____

_____

_____

Prayer

Jesus, only You can satisfy. Help me to see the signs of spiritual and physical hunger. Teach me to come to You for what I need. Amen.

What's Next?

This Jesus, delivered up according to the definite plan and foreknowledge of God…
—ACTS 2:23 (ESV)

"Ten more minutes and it will be time to clean up."
"Five more minutes and it will be time to clean up."
"Two more minutes and it will be time to clean up."
"One more minute. . ."

Miss Haley finished up her countdown and looked around the room. Before she had even made it to one minute, most students had folded up the games and put away their art supplies. She had learned the hard way what happens when students aren't ready to move on to the next activity, triggered by a sudden change they didn't see coming.

Haley knew most of the kids in the program had experienced trauma. She knew about the three foster homes Daniel had already lived in, and the way the social worker had shown up at school unexpectedly with the news he wouldn't be going home again. She knew the story of Uma's mom—the tragic sudden death nobody could have predicted. Her room was full of hard stories, and they came rushing back to her students' minds anytime they experienced an unexpected change, even if it was only to move from an art activity to reading time.

After so much unexpected and unwanted change, each student was desperate for predictability. While she wasn't in control of everything and some transitions were unavoidable, she knew she could at least give a warning. So "the countdown" became one of her routines. The gentle warning and reminder that transition was on its way calmed the anxiety of her students and smoothed away the frequent outbursts of the past.

As a general rule, we *all* feel calmer when we know what to expect or what's coming next. Warnings about upcoming transitions lower fear and anxiety associated with unanticipated change. Similarly, felt safety is increased when we share information, such as an order of events or expectations in an unfamiliar place.

In Jesus's final days on Earth, He warned His disciples what was about to happen to Him. They may not have fully understood His message, but that didn't change His intention. Jesus was giving them information about what would happen next.

> *From that time on Jesus began to explain to his disciples that he must go to Jerusalem and suffer many things at the hands of the elders, the chief priests and the teachers of the law, and that he must be killed and on the third day be raised to life.*
>
> — MATTHEW 16:21

Later, after encountering the risen Savior, Jesus' disciples found renewed strength knowing Jesus prepared them ahead of time for what was to come. Even today we can feel safe about what's still to come.

- Jesus conquered death, is preparing a place for us, and will come back for us (John 14:3).
- He will make all things new (Revelation 21:5) and we will live with Him forever.
- There will be a new heaven and a new earth—Eden restored—and His children *"will need no light of lamp or sun, for the Lord God will be their light, and they will reign forever and ever"* (Revelation 22:1–5, ESV).

As followers of Jesus, we can find peace and safety in the predictability of our story's ending. We are not left wandering in the darkness unsure of where we are headed. God has shared the plan with us, given us His Son as the path to get there, and secured our future with Him.

Trauma-informed Tip

The majority of behavioral breakdowns happen in transition.[24] We can ease transitions and avoid meltdowns by giving warnings. Start with a ten-minute warning before ending or changing activities. It's important to be near and make eye contact rather than simply yelling a warning across the room. Next, give a five-minute, two-minute, then one-minute warning. Once the countdown has ended, help everyone wrap up and move onto the next activity. When transitioning to something new, like visiting a new place or introducing a brand-new activity, give as much information as possible. These two strategies will increase felt safety and lower fear and anxiety.

---

1. What causes me to feel anxious or unsafe?
2. Scripture explains what we can expect on earth and in heaven. Of those expectations, what do I look forward to?
3. Do I know anyone who struggles with being anxious, especially when encountering new or unpredictable events? What can I do to help increase their feeling of safety?

_____

_____

_____

_____

_____

_____

_____

_____

_____

_____

_____

_____

_____

_____

_____

_____

_____

_____

Prayer

Jesus, I want to walk with You so that when You say left, we go left and when You say stop, we stop. Help me to trust you with the plan for my life. Amen.

The Power of a Routine

He went to Nazareth, where he had been brought up, and on the Sabbath day he went into the synagogue, as was his custom.

— LUKE 4:16

From the outside, life looked perfect for Sarah. She lived in a great house in a great neighborhood and her parents were well-respected throughout the community—especially her Dad, who was affectionately known as "the good doctor." However, on the inside, life was anything but. People didn't know that inside that pretty house, Sarah was being abused by her dad. When she was almost nine years old, it all poured out when the school nurse, a safe adult in Sarah's life, began asking questions. That's what led to Sarah's foster placement with the Goldbergs.

At first, Sarah felt ashamed, alone, and, most of all, afraid. More than ever, she used a protective strategy called "acting in"—withdrawing inward as a way to protect herself from the necessity of healthy relationships. It worked with Mr. and Mrs. Goldberg and their two younger daughters, who found themselves struggling to make an initial attachment with Sarah. Sarah believed if she faded into the background and made herself invisible, this superpower would keep her safe. Only it wasn't a superpower. It caused Sarah to become more withdrawn, sad, isolated, and unable to receive the healing Jesus wanted to provide her through the Goldbergs.

The Goldbergs realized they needed to help Sarah *feel* safe so she could become truly "powerful." One primary way they equipped Sarah was by creating a weekly calendar. They asked for her input, and Sarah helped decide a routine for:

- what happened after school
- when to expect family dinner
- a predictable set of events at bedtime
- the schedule for soccer practice, church, and the other activities she and the family were involved in

Among the many strategies the Goldbergs employed, the predictability of routine activities slowly empowered Sarah. Her anxiety decreased, and she came out of the shell she built through her "acting in" strategy. Now knowing the rhythm of her life, Sarah felt safe to connect with Mr. and Mrs. Goldberg and their daughters.

Isn't this something the Father offers to each of us? While it's true that

"it is for freedom that Christ has set us free"

— GALATIANS 5:1

and we

"are not under the law, but under grace"

— ROMANS 6:14

The Father invites us into a routine so we are empowered to take on the unpredictability and anxieties of the world.

The routine? The Sabbath, a regular, predictable rhythm where we set everything aside to reconnect with Him and find space to restore our souls. The Sabbath is not a day to *recover* and hide from the effects of being in the world, but it is a day each week where the Lord *empowers* us for the work ahead. What a glorious gift!

Whether you've experienced life-altering trauma like Sarah or are struggling with other pressures, Sabbath was made *for* you (Mark 2:27). Our Heavenly Father waits to engage you there. *His* predictable routine is meant for *your* healing and restoration.

Trauma-informed Tip

Increase felt safety by establishing and maintaining a consistent routine. For example, a daily schedule at home may include wake up, brush teeth, eat breakfast, go to school, come home from school, eat a snack, do homework, eat dinner, play, shower, go to bed. When followed daily, this simple order of events increases predictability and feelings of safety. Create weekly and monthly schedules with any upcoming special events or out-of-the-ordinary activities. Review the plans together and then display daily, weekly, and monthly schedules in a visible location so everyone can review and reference them when needed.

1. What am I currently doing that could be shifted to set aside time for a regular Sabbath with God?
2. What do I expect Sabbath to look like? What do I expect to get out of it?
3. What is a creative way to engage the kids in my life in making a predictable routine for them?

_____

_____

_____

_____

_____

_____

_____

_____

_____

_____

_____

_____

_____

_____

_____

_____

_____

_____

_____

_____

_____

Prayer

Jesus, I want to have the discipline to set aside regularly time with You. Help me to understand the power of a healthy, Spirit-filled routine. Amen.

This week, what did I learn about myself? Others? The Lord?

_____
_____
_____
_____
_____
_____
_____
_____
_____
_____
_____
_____
_____
_____
_____
_____
_____
_____
_____
_____
_____
_____
_____
_____
_____
_____

I am the vine; you are the branches. The one who remains in me and I in him produces much fruit, because you can do nothing without me.

— JOHN 15:5 (CSB) —

Week 6

Connection Matters

Apart from a connection to the vine, there is no fruit. In our spiritual lives, connection with God is how we receive what we need from Him, *and* it's how we produce the fruit He wants of us. Connection to the vine is essential to life. Alone and isolated, we can do nothing! But, how do we stay connected when the gap feels wide? When the distance between us and God feels too great?

This week we will look at the power of connections formed and voices restored. We will see the power of yes and how it speaks to unconditional approval.

Give Voice

*And if we know that he hears us—whatever we ask
—we know that we have what we asked of him.*

— 1 JOHN 5:15

By the time he arrived at the after-school program, Michael was having a terrible day. He'd missed recess as a consequence for yelling at a girl in class. What the teacher hadn't heard was the mean comment Blair made *first.*

Was he just supposed to just take it?

"You're so stupid your own parents don't want to take care of you," she whispered. "If I'm so stupid, why do I bring my homework every day and you don't?!" he yelled back.

He tried to tell the teacher Blair started it, but she wouldn't let him explain. He was always the "bad one", so she assumed it was his fault again. Michael glared at Blair as she skipped out of the classroom to play with the other kids.

After a day like that, the last thing he wanted to do was homework. He sat down with his tutor Anna and tossed his notebook on the desk. "I'm not doing anything today," he announced.

Undeterred, Anna opened his notebook and read the instructions. "'Write a paragraph introducing yourself to the class. ' Okay, let's start with just one thing about you."

"I hate school!" Michael shouted.

Without flinching, Anna responded, "That's a great start. Write that sentence." Surprised, he wrote, *My name is Michael and I hate school.*

Rather than silence his comment as "too negative" or "inappropriate," Anna turned up the volume on Michael's voice and listened to what he was trying to express.

Feeling heard for the first time that day, Michael told Anna all about the unfair situation with Blair. As he did, he felt the pressure of the day melting away. He completed the paragraph in his notebook and eventually felt so excited to share it that he decided to remove the words "and I hate school" and replace them with "and I love Fortnite!"

One of the many losses children experience because of early childhood trauma is the loss of their "voice." Early experiences of abuse and neglect teach children it isn't safe to ask for what they need or to express what they feel. Thankfully, what has been lost *can* be restored.

We restore voice when we invite others to share their desires, hopes, and dreams, even if they are different from our own.

We restore voice when we create a safe place to share fears and anxieties without judgment or condemnation.

We restore voice when we allow others to weigh in on a decision, even when it doesn't end up being the easiest or shortest path.

Biblically, there are countless places where God honors a person's voice.

- Throughout the Psalms, God makes room for the many emotions of the Psalmist—highs and lows, fears and praise.
- In the Old Testament, Job vents his pain and frustration to God, who doesn't flinch; Jonah complains about God's compassion toward Nineveh and God doesn't silence him; and Moses expresses his fears about being unqualified to do what God is asking.
- In the New Testament, Jesus gives voice to the mother of John and James to make a request; He gives voice to Mary and Martha as they grieve the death of their brother; and He gives voice to Nicodemus, who questions the very foundation of what he was taught his entire life.

Restoring the voice of earnest seekers is a theme throughout Jesus' ministry. God invites *us* to cry out to Him, reassuring us He will listen. He gives each of us a voice in our times of requesting, questioning, and grief.

Let's commit to being restorers of other's voices as we follow His example.

Trauma-informed Tip

Giving voice is allowing a child to express their thoughts, feelings, opinions, questions, and dreams in a safe and inviting space, even if it is unpleasant to hear.[25] The next time a child or teen says something you disagree with or dislike, rather than ignore the comment or tell them not to say it, try asking more questions to understand their heart and create space for their voice to be heard. The next time you are planning an event or activity, ask the children or teens what they think you should do. For example, when meal planning at home, invite their opinions about what you should make for dinner that week.

1. When have I felt like my voice wasn't heard? How did I respond?
2. How do I feel knowing God wants me to express my desires, questions, and pain to Him?
3. What is one thing I can do to become a better listener? How can I empower someone to use their voice?

_____

_____

_____

_____

_____

_____

_____

_____

_____

_____

_____

_____

_____

_____

_____

_____

_____

_____

_____

_____

_____

Prayer

*Jesus, thank you for hearing me! I am so grateful
to have a Father who listens. Amen.*

I See You

I call on the Lord in my distress, and he answers me.
— PSALM 120:1

Jeremiah did not want to go outside with his class. The rest of the students lined up single file and quietly proceeded to the playground. Jeremiah melted to the floor, rolled back and forth a few times, and then settled facedown, refusing to make eye contact with anyone around him.

Nora had seen this before. She knew that demanding he "just get up" or threatening a consequence would not work. She decided to try a different approach and sat down on the floor by his side. "I wonder what color Jeremiah's eyes are…" she playfully wondered out loud. "Do you think they're purple? What about orange?"

Jeremiah slowly turned his head to the side, peeking through his barely spread fingers to make eye contact with her, a small smile forming, despite his efforts to remain serious. "Oh! What beautiful brown eyes you have!" she proclaimed.

The small smile burst open into a giggle, and Jeremiah's defenses came tumbling down.

Jeremiah making intentional eye contact with a trusted adult was the beginning of his connection with her. Once he felt connected, he was more open to Nora's gentle guidance to choose a game and join the other students outside. Connection comes first.

Eye contact is a powerful connector. It has the power to change brain chemistry and wordlessly establish a basis of trust.

There is so much that can be communicated in a look, a glance, or a gaze.

With only our eyes we can say…

"I see you."
"I'm on your side."
"I care about you."
"You have my attention."

The apostle Peter knew something about the power of eye contact. In Matthew 14, Jesus calls Peter to Him while walking on the water. Peter takes the first few steps with his eyes locked on Jesus. But as soon as the wind picks up, his eyes and his attention pull elsewhere.

And Peter answered him, "Lord, if it is you, command me to come to you on the water." He said, "Come." So Peter got out of the boat and walked on the water and came to Jesus. But when he saw the wind, he was afraid, and beginning to sink he cried out, "Lord, save me."

— MATTHEW 14:28–31

Peter turned his attention to the wind and waves and began to sink. In a certain way, we are no different. When we are unsure of ourselves or our surroundings, making eye contact with someone who has shown us they are trustworthy creates a bridge.

In Psalm 121, the Psalmist intentionally puts his eyes on the mountains, establishing and reaffirming his connection with the Lord.

I lift up my eyes to the mountains—
where does my help come from?
My help comes from the Lord,
the maker of heaven and earth.

— PSALM 121:1–2

Where our eyes go matters.

Making healthy eye contact positively changes brain chemistry by providing a healthy spike in dopamine.[26] It also promotes learning. However, sustained eye contact may be challenging for some children with a history of trauma, so don't expect too much at once. When communicating something important or reinforcing a loving connection, gently ask for eye contact by saying, "Hey, can I see those beautiful eyes of yours?" or "Can you give me eyes please?"

1. When I make intentional eye contact with someone I trust, how does it make me feel?
2. Do I believe that God is near enough to make eye contact with me? If I had God's full attention, what would I say to Him?
3. Who in my life needs to be reassured they are seen? Try asking to see their eyes in a gentle and inviting way.

*Lord, I turn my face towards You. I look to You
for guidance and significance. I love you. Amen.*

Already Approved

For am I now seeking the approval of man, or of God? Or am I trying to please man? If I were still trying to please man, I would not be a servant of Christ.

— GALATIANS 1:10 (ESV)

Dana burst through the door brimming with confidence and elation. She couldn't wait to share the news that for the first time all year, she was included in the teacher's Friday newsletter as an "outstanding student". This coveted list includes students who have completed all of their assignments and attended school every day that week. It had been six weeks since Dana last attended a full week of school, and her failing grades were evidence of the many assignments left incomplete. This public proclamation of approval was a victory, a title she had secretly longed for but never received.

The path to victory began long before the Friday newsletter arrived. Unfortunately, in her early life, negative words and experiences built a belief system declaring she would never be anything but ordinary. However, over time, something shifted in her as a result of the constant refrain of her tutor, Tash, whose encouraging words and consistent presence sounded like this:

"I love spending time with you!"
"I'm here to help when things get hard."
"I'm so happy you're here!"

Dana came to believe she was worthy and could be outstanding. Her inclusion in the Friday newsletter only reinforced this belief.

We can spend energy trying to *win* God's approval by doing the "right things." Or, as committed Christ followers, we can *rest* in His unconditional approval.

The beauty of the latter option? This unconditional approval has the power to unlock something deep within us. John 1:12 tells us,

> *Yet to all who did receive him, to those who believed in his name, he gave the right to become children of God.*

We're a part of God's family! He approves of us so much He identifies us as His children.

You can find God's unconditional love for us throughout the Old and New Testaments. In just one chapter of Romans, the apostle Paul describes three different times how God approves of us.

> *While we were still weak Christ died for the ungodly.*
> — ROMANS 5:6

> *While we were still sinners, Christ died for us.*
> — ROMANS 5:8

> *If while we were enemies we were reconciled to God by the death of his Son.*
> — ROMANS 5:10

Christ's sacrifice on the cross is proof of the value He gives us. He doesn't withhold love or approval based on how we miss the mark of what we should be. In fact, he loves and approves of us *because of what He did on our behalf*, and this gives us the freedom and confidence to love Him and others as He has loved us.

When we live knowing we are already approved of, it changes everything.

Trauma-informed Tip

Children and teens from hard places often have negative self-images and deep feelings of failure. The critical job of safe adults is to counteract negative self-perception by communicating approval. Remind them, "I like being with you. You're such a great kid," even—maybe *more* importantly—when undesirable behavior is on display. Communicate the difference between disapproving of their behavior and approving of them as people. Try something like, "What just happened is not ok. I approve of *you*. I just don't approve of what happened. We can fix this together."

1. How much do I give and withhold approval of others based on their behavior?
2. What does the Bible say about how God continues to approve of me even while I am sinning?
3. How can I model God's way to others?

_____

_____

_____

_____

_____

_____

_____

_____

_____

_____

_____

_____

_____

_____

_____

_____

_____

_____

_____

_____

_____

Prayer

Jesus, it can be so hard when we look around and wonder who sees us and what they think of us. Help me have eyes only for You. I want to understand what it really means to be known and loved by You. Amen.

Presence as a Gift

Let us come into His presence with thanksgiving;
let us make a joyful noise to Him with songs of praise.
— PSALM 95:2 (ESV)

Soccer games, track meets, school assemblies, choir concerts, graduations, weddings… What these events have in common is an audience. We've all been audience members or, sometimes, the star of the show. When we're on stage, we scan the crowd looking for *our* people, listening for their voices, waving when we find them. When we're in the audience, we show up to watch and celebrate the people we hold dear. We love them and our very presence is a non-verbal, "*I see you.*"

For Jack, his moment as the star was junior high graduation. As the students excitedly took their seats, Jack made eye contact with a teacher in the crowd and mouthed the question, "My mom?"

He scanned every corner and couldn't find her. It had been years since they lived under the same roof, and she had never been to one of his soccer games, birthday parties, or school celebrations. Their relationship was mending however, and she promised not to miss this one.

For children who have spent time separated from a parent, presence matters. Years of separation have whispered the message, *You are alone and no one is coming for you.*

Jack's teacher couldn't help but notice the ache in his eyes as he searched the room. The ceremony started and all she could do was pray his mom would show up, that this time she would be there to cheer for him. With just ten minutes left in the ceremony, she saw Jack's mom sneak in the back and quickly waved her over. Jack's mom told his teacher about a three-hour bus ride to get there and a one-hour walk through the neighborhood trying to find the school. She was frazzled and frustrated, but *present*. When the ceremony ended, Jack went straight to his teacher for a congratulatory hug and before he pulled away, she whispered, "Look who's here!"

The big, brave, 15-year-old boy hugged his mom and wept. She showed up! She cheered him on! She was present! Her presence said what he needed to hear: "You are known and loved, and I came for you."

Have you ever considered your presence a gift? It doesn't cost money or require fancy wrapping, but it might mean more than any item you put in a box. When we consider the many gifts God has given us, His presence tops the list. Time with Him is a privilege He offers us over and over again.

Moses understood that and would go into the tent where, as Exodus 33:11 says,

> *The Lord would speak to Moses face to face, as one speaks to a friend.*

This is the kind of intimate presence God offers. It goes on to say,

> *Then Moses would return to the camp, but his young*
> *aide Joshua son of Nun did not leave the tent.*

The young student of Moses followed him into God's presence and didn't want to leave! It could be argued that it's what gave Joshua the courage to accomplish all he would later be known for. He understood the power of being in God's presence. Let's celebrate God's presence in our lives as one of His greatest gifts!

When we show up for "our people"—offering strength, love, and support—it is a precious gift that comes with the added bonus of bringing God's presence with us as well.

Trauma-informed Tip

In the hustle and bustle of daily life, it's easy to forget presence is one of the greatest gifts we can give. Prioritize showing up in moments both big and small. Remember your presence matters more than any other gift.

———

1. When has someone "showed up" for me in a small or big way? Why was it important to me that they were there?
2. Where in Scripture do I see Jesus setting aside time to be in the presence of His father? Why was this time so important to Jesus, and what did He receive as a result?
3. Who are two or three people I can be present with this week? What does "showing up" for each of them look like?

_____
_____
_____
_____
_____
_____
_____
_____
_____
_____
_____
_____
_____
_____
_____
_____
_____
_____
_____
_____
_____
_____
_____

Prayer

Lord, if I had nothing in life but You, it would be enough.
Your presence is a gift I can enjoy all the time.
Help me bring Your presence into the rooms where I am. Amen.

Yes. Yes. Yes.

"Can I have a piece of gum?" Anna asked with a strong, clear voice from the backseat of the car.

"Yes, of course you can!" answered her tutor excitedly, pride and joy on display in her huge smile.

Every Monday as Anna climbed in the back of the car, she stared at the bucket of Double Bubble gum. Unbeknownst to her, the gum was meant to create an opportunity for her to hear the word "Yes!" Initially, she was too nervous to ask for a piece, not trusting the two new people picking her up for a summer reading program. She would stare at the bucket during the entire ride. It took some time before she learned the gum was there for kids, and she could ask if she wanted some.

A few Mondays into the program, Anna decided to take a risk. She quietly said from the back seat, "I know you're probably going to say no, but could I have a piece of gum?" She braced herself because her past had taught her that adults say no when you want something. But the interaction didn't go the way so many others had.

Anna's voice was heard and the response came, "Yes, of course you can!"
With a yes, trust formed.

We are biologically wired as humans to build a bond of trust when someone tells us yes. A typical newborn baby from a healthy environment hears a heartfelt yes hundreds of times a day.

"Yes, I will feed you."
"Yes, I will change your diaper."
"Yes, I will rock you to sleep."

Every yes fills a piggy bank of trust between child and caregiver, creating a balance to withstand the moments when a parent has to say no.

For children and teens with a history of trauma, their account is in the negative. They don't have a growing piggy bank of trust. But we can intentionally make deposits into their overdrawn accounts. "Yes" is a powerful word that satisfies something deeper than just the desire of the moment. Yes to a piece of gum for Anna says, "I'm for you. I hear you. What you want matters to me."

God wired us this way, knowing the power of yes and how it builds trust. 2 Corinthians 1:20 says,

> *For all of God's promises have been fulfilled in Christ with a resounding "Yes!"*
> *And through Christ, our "Amen" ascends to God for his glory.*

God is sovereign, so He knows when to say yes to us and when what we are hoping to hear isn't in our best interest. Thankfully, God doesn't say yes to every request we bring to Him, but He does give us the ultimate yes through Jesus.

By sending his Son to die for us, God said:

- *Yes! I see you and your need for salvation.*
- *Yes! I hear you when you pray and you matter to Me.*
- *Yes! Every promise I made is for you too.*

He fills our "yes banks" with His faithfulness, and the result is a growing account of connection between us.

Trauma-informed Tip

Try saying yes today to something safe and reasonable that a child or teen in your life would like to do. When you do have to say no, try reframing so it is received as a yes. Rather than, "No, you can't play soccer." Try instead, "I know it would be so fun to play soccer. We can play after you finish your homework."

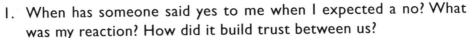

1. When has someone said yes to me when I expected a no? What was my reaction? How did it build trust between us?
2. What yes am I hearing from God right now (or have I heard from Him in the past) that is meant to build trust between us?
3. Who have I had the joy of saying yes to when they were expecting a no? How was our relationship strengthened?

_____

_____

_____

_____

_____

_____

_____

_____

_____

_____

_____

_____

_____

_____

_____

_____

_____

_____

_____

_____

Prayer

Lord, thank you for all the times You've said yes to me. Thank you for how it affirms You are listening. I want to say yes to you too. Yes, I will go. Yes, I will listen. Yes, Lord. Amen.

This week, what did I learn about myself? Others? The Lord?

_____

_____

_____

_____

_____

_____

_____

_____

_____

_____

_____

_____

_____

_____

_____

_____

_____

_____

_____

_____

_____

_____

_____

_____

_____

_____

_____

_____

_____

_____

Train up a child in the way he should go;
even when he is old he will not depart from it.

— PROVERBS 25:5–7 (ESV) —

Correction Matters

God is clear in Scripture that there is a *way we should go*, a narrow path leading to righteousness. Some choices lead to health and flourishing, while other choices lead to death and destruction. Finding and then remaining on the way is *against* our nature; we must be taught, trained, corrected, and led.

This week we will look at how God leads and corrects us and how, in turn, we can lead and correct others. We will learn new strategies tailored to the unique needs of children who have experienced trauma and discover the way those strategies mirror God's own heart for us.

Given What We Don't Deserve

In him we have redemption through his blood, the forgiveness of sins, in accordance with the riches of God's grace.

— EPHESIANS 1:7

"**R**achel, something is going on with Steven's bank account," Chris said after checking his son's balance. Steven had been working three jobs all summer and was saving for his school year. Chris was looking to see what had accumulated from his efforts.

"There's nothing there, and he's overdrawn." *What could he possibly have bought worth three months of paychecks?*

Chris went looking for Steven, and a terrible story unfolded; he was the victim of a convincing phishing scheme. Someone pretending to be from his new college emailed looking for a dog walker. They had pictures and were skilled at executing their con. Steven was hooked and gave the scammer more information than he should have. Now all his money was gone.

Steven was crushed—broken, really. Every side job, second job, difficult job he had accepted over the summer resulted in nothing. Every time he had said no to a friend in order to pick up another shift… all the money was gone. On top of that, he felt embarrassed, stupid, angry, and ashamed.

A couple days later, Chris was wrestling with his parental responsibility in all of it. He thought about the similarities to when we get in over our heads and are afraid or ashamed to ask for help as adults. How could he and Rachel use this situation to give Steven a glimpse into how God works?

They sat Steven down. He had spent the last two days with a brave face, but it was covering a broken heart. "Steven," Chris began, "I want to let you know your Mom and I are going to reimburse you for what was stolen." Steven's head snapped up and he looked confused, yet already relieved. Chis continued, "I want you to remember this moment for the rest of your life. We were given what we didn't deserve from our heavenly Father, and we are called to look like Him to you. We want more than anything for you to grasp this idea: our Father delights in giving us back what is lost. He loves you, and in Him, you are not defined by your mistakes."

It was a holy moment, a redemptive exchange that will pay dividends in Steven's life worth far more than the dollars it cost his parents.

Hebrews 4:15 says,

> *We do not have a high priest who is unable to sympathize with our weaknesses.*

God sees our struggles and understands when we fall. He isn't waiting to rub it in our faces, but offers grace freely to all who ask. In the same way, we can use teachable moments to demonstrate how powerful God's love is.

It's easy to fall into a pattern of thinking that "the punishment must fit the crime", or "do the crime, do the time". Instead, when we give undeserved grace, we follow in the footsteps of our Father.

> *For the wages of sin is death, but the free gift of God is eternal life in Christ Jesus our Lord.*
> — ROMANS 6:23 (ESV)

Our sinful actions left us deserving of death, but God changed the story. He gives us what we don't deserve. This is the foundation we stand on as we correct the mistakes and missteps of others.

Children and teens who have experienced trauma are well-versed in harsh and inappropriate punishments at the hands of caregivers. Because of this, many traditional discipline strategies will not be effective and can actually make things worse. Traditional discipline strategies include physical punishment, long and intense verbal communication, and isolation. Most of us probably experienced some combination of these with our own parents and will instinctively use them with children and teens in our lives.

- Instead of physical punishment, offer appropriate structure and empathetic nurturing.
- Instead of consequences, offer a chance to do it over.
- Instead of isolation, connect with a child before you correct them.

Change in behavior is possible when we open our minds to new tools and remember the grace so lavishly poured out on us by our Father.

Trauma-informed Tip

Take time to reflect on which discipline strategies you experienced as a child. Be mindful of when you are likely to use these strategies with children and teens in your life today. The next time you find yourself focused on punishing negative behavior rather than teaching positive behavior, stop and shift your perspective. Ask how you can give undeserved grace in this moment and teach rather than punish.

1. How was discipline enforced in my life growing up? How has this affected my current view of discipline?
2. When has God shown me grace and mercy when I didn't deserve it?
3. What forms of discipline do I want to change/incorporate in my interactions with children and teens?

_____

_____

_____

_____

_____

_____

_____

_____

_____

_____

_____

_____

_____

_____

_____

_____

_____

_____

_____

_____

_____

_____

Prayer

Jesus, thank you for the grace You've extended to me. I don't deserve the blessing and gifts You offer me daily, yet I receive them humbly. Amen.

Try It Again

Who saved us and called us to a holy calling, not because of our works but because of his own purpose and grace, which he gave us in Christ Jesus before the ages began.

— 2 TIMOTHY 1:9 (ESV)

"Let's try that again," he said for what felt like the hundredth time. Nine-year old Jeremiah was trying every last bit of his foster dad's patience. This time it was his backpack, flung across the room and landing *near* the shelf where it belonged. Almost the right place, but definitely the wrong way to get there.

Two months ago, Jeremiah's dad would have lost his temper, frustrated at having to correct the same behavior as yesterday, the day before, and the day before that. But losing his temper would have inevitably led them down a predictable path, with Jeremiah then using disrespectful words and having a total meltdown. The whole afternoon would have been derailed, filled with frustrated looks and angry body language until bedtime.

That would not be the story today. Armed with newfound knowledge, this foster dad's perspective was changing. He took a deep breath, decided to try something new, and calmly and playfully asked Jeremiah to "try it again".

He gave him a re-do—the opportunity to try something again when Jeremiah didn't get it right the first time. This calm reminder averted a crisis and became a new tool in Dad's tool belt.

A natural instinct in the face of undesirable behavior is to call it out as "bad," and then give a consequence for the action. In some cases, this strategy works to correct the immediate situation and prevent the behavior next time. However, it's missing a crucial step: practice.

When we repeat a behavior, a pathway is formed in the brain, like a road that becomes familiar.[27] Done often enough, the body then follows as if on autopilot. Have you ever moved the location of a kitchen appliance? For days after its relocation, your brain and body will instinctively take you to the old spot, following the path it's used many times before. It takes an intentional pause and an intentional re-do to teach your brain and body the right way to go.

Children and teens who have experienced early childhood trauma have well-worn paths for undesirable behavior in their brains. These protective strategies that were essential for surviving traumatic experiences are familiar and instinctual. If we never give children the opportunity to practice good behavior and forge a new path in their brain, we are working against brain science. We are drawing attention to what they *shouldn't* do and not giving the brain and body the experience of success.

Throughout Scripture, God gives His children the opportunity to try things again when they didn't get it right the first time.

- When Jonah fled rather than follow God's call to Nineveh, God sent a fish to swallow him up. God said, "Let's try it again."
- When Peter denied Jesus three times, Jesus met him on the beach and asked him three times, "Do you love me?" God offered, "Let's try it again."
- When Paul was bent on persecuting and killing Christians, God struck him blind on the road to Damascus and he received mercy from followers of Christ. God led him to try it again.
- When we sin—going our own way or seeking glory for ourselves—God calls us to repent. He strengthens us to try it again.

New pathways can be forged in the brain, creating roads for "good behavior" that pleases and glorifies God. When we inevitably mess up (because we are human and works in progress), God says to us,

"Let's try it again."

Trauma-informed Tip

When you see a child or teen misbehave, offer a re-do. Rather than immediately giving a consequence or launching into a long explanation of what they did wrong, simply say, "Hey, let's try that again." Additionally, try empowering children and teens to *ask* for a re-do if they recognize they have messed up and want to try again.

1. Where has God given me a re-do in life? How can I thank Him for that today?
2. How can God's offer of redemption encourage me to offer the same to the kids in my life?
3. What are the benefits of giving someone a re-do?

_____

_____

_____

_____

_____

_____

_____

_____

_____

_____

_____

_____

_____

_____

_____

_____

_____

_____

_____

_____

Prayer

*God, You are always offering me a re-do. Thank you for Your grace towards me.
I want to extend that grace to others. Help me to look like You. Amen.*

Relationship First

*Yet to all who did receive him, who believed in his
name, he gave the right to become children of God.*

— JOHN 1:12

She sat on the couch, unmoving. It was an hour past bedtime, and Sigu was *not* going to give in. She had wanted to go to the birthday party, the one where all of her friends were going to sleep over and play video games all night. But her foster mom had said no, giving some excuse about laws and rules and licensed caregivers. Sigu had stopped listening after the no. She didn't care about anything else. Disappointment and sadness quickly gave way to rage and a stubborn refusal to do anything her foster mom asked. She sat on the couch, not looking at her, and acting like no one else even existed. *No way* she was giving up this fight.

Exasperated and exhausted, Deborah managed to get the other kids to bed even while dancing around Sigu's angry glares. Now the house was dark and in the quiet, Sigu sat frozen.

It's time to lay down the hammer, Deborah thought, listing all the threats she could make and privileges she could remove. Just before launching into her counterattack though, a small voice echoed in her head, *connect before you correct.* The last thing she wanted was to connect with the kid who had rudely ignored her for the last three hours. Deborah breathed deeply, counted to ten, and reminded herself the end goal was heart-change and healing, not compliance.

Instead of listing threats, Deborah plopped down next to Sigu and said, "Oh no, Sigu's frozen. She must be a popsicle. I wonder what flavor she is. Maybe orange, that's my favorite. I hope it's orange…" It was slight, but Deborah didn't miss it—

Sigu's eyes shifted, she cracked a slight smile, and she met Deborah's kind and loving gaze.

"Oh, hey. There you are. I've *missed* you."

In John 8, we read how Jesus approaches a woman caught in adultery. Everyone surrounding her didn't see *her*, but they saw her sin. They were willing to condemn her without a conversation. Jesus was more interested in showing the crowd (and the teachers within it) how to love than He was in correcting the woman's behavior.

> *Jesus bent down and started to write on the ground with his finger. When they kept on questioning him, he straightened up and said to them, "Let any one of you who is without sin be the first to throw a stone at her." Again he stooped down and wrote on the ground.*
>
> *At this, those who heard began to go away one at a time, the older ones first, until only Jesus was left, with the woman still standing there. Jesus straightened up and asked her, "Woman, where are they? Has no one condemned you?" "No one, sir," she said. "Then neither do I condemn you," Jesus declared. "Go now and leave your life of sin."*
>
> — JOHN 8:6–11

Correction reaches the deepest depths of the heart only when it stands on the foundation of connection. Before all else, God calls us to be in relationship with Him.

- Rules without relationship will inevitably lead to rebellion.
- Relationship moves hearts and transforms lives.

When we are in need of correction, let's remember we are children of God, and He is ready to connect with us before He corrects.

Connection before correction can look and sound many different ways. It could be a playful comment, a gentle hug, or even a direct reminder you are on the same team. When responding to misbehavior, rather than sending the child or teen away from you (e.g., a traditional "time out"), seek proximity and connection. Try a "time in", sitting near or remaining within eyesight of a child or teen while they take time to calm down. Once they have, *then* calmly address the behavior.

1. When have I experienced the opposite of today's topic (i.e., correction before connection)? How did that make me feel?
2. In what ways does God show me He is "sitting near" or "remaining within eyesight"? How can I enjoy a "time in" with Him?
3. What is my natural instinct: connection or correction? How can I do both—moving toward a child or teen to improve connection and then offering necessary correction?

_____
_____
_____
_____
_____
_____
_____
_____
_____
_____
_____
_____
_____
_____
_____
_____
_____
_____
_____

Prayer

Jesus, You teach us relationship is worth protecting. You demonstrate sticking with us, even when we are sinful. Thank you for Your grace, Amen.

Structure & Nurture

"The goal is to build a contraption allowing your egg to survive when we throw it off the second floor balcony." The students' eyes widened and they protested, "How is that possible?"

"I have two boxes here, one full of soft, fluffy, gentle materials and another full of hard, rigid, sturdy materials. In order for your egg to survive the fall, it will need both."

The students went to work alternating between the soft box and the hard one, balancing the ratio, giving their eggs what they needed to survive. Then came the moment of truth, the toss. One by one they threw their egg vessels off the balcony. Many eggs met the hard floor with a splat. But some—nestled inside the right balance of soft and hard materials—survived intact!

As they gathered around to reflect, the teacher introduced new words for the two boxes. Rather than *soft* and *hard*, she called them *nurture* and *structure*. "In order for your eggs to survive, they needed the balance of both nurture and structure materials. For people to survive and grow in a healthy way, we also need both nurture and structure. Let's think of your own lives. What are some examples of soft nurture your parents give you?"

Hands shot in the air. "Hugs… I love you's… Presents!"

"And what about structure?"

The class shouted out, "Curfews... Chores... Rules."

"That's right!" the teacher affirmed. "When an adult gives you both nurture and structure, they provide what you need to survive and grow. Too much of one, and, like the eggs, we can break under pressure."

The right balance of nurture and structure leads to healthy and thriving kids and teens, but finding that balance can be hard. God doesn't leave us without an example to follow. It's His very nature to be loving, merciful, and nurturing, while also establishing boundaries and expectations for how we live. He is the perfect balance of nurture and structure.

From the very beginning, we see this balance in action. Genesis 3 narrates Adam and Eve's sin against God—disobeying the only rule of the garden by eating from the tree of the knowledge of good and evil. They violated the structure God created for them—structure meant to keep them safe, connected, and flourishing. After pronouncing the consequences for this disobedience, God does something unexpected.

> *The Lord God made garments of skin for Adam and his wife and clothed them.*
> — GENESIS 3:21

In the middle of this moment, when new structures, new limits, and new consequences are revealed, God still provides nurture. He sees their nakedness and *clothes them*. In the middle of their consequence, one brought on by their own actions, this compassionate God gives a gift to protect them on the journey ahead.

Trauma-informed Tip

Research shows kids raised by parents who balance high nurture with high structure grow up to be the most successful adults.[28] They are more likely to be happy and self-disciplined and are less likely to rebel in adolescence. Find ways to balance both approaches, even if you are naturally drawn to one over the other. Establish boundaries and enforce them. Create predictable schedules and routines. Communicate love, pride, and excitement. Listen well and give children the chance to express themselves. In these ways, you create structure *and* nurture.

1. How did I experience nurturing in my childhood? How did I experience structure?
2. What is one Scripture passage that points to God as a nurturer? As giving structure?
3. Based on those Scripture passages, how can I be more like Jesus and provide nurture and structure to someone?

_____

_____

_____

_____

_____

_____

_____

_____

_____

_____

_____

_____

_____

_____

_____

_____

_____

_____

_____

Prayer

Jesus, You are the perfect parent, balancing nurture and structure in a way that supports and corrects. Teach me to model You and reveal where I am out of balance. Amen.

Learning How To Live

Love must be sincere. Detest what is evil. Cling to what is good. Be devoted to one
another in brotherly love... Be joyful in hope, patient in affliction, persistent
in prayer. Share with the saints who are in need. Practice hospitality.

— ROMANS 12:9–10, 12–13

Brandy, who had training and experience in trauma-informed care, left her small group materials unattended in the gym in order to retrieve additional supplies from her car. While she was gone, a group of kids entered the gym to play basketball and blow off steam. When she returned, she walked into the start of a fight erupting at the far end of the gym.

Thirteen-year-old Jumari, a club regular, and fourteen-year-old Delon, new to the after school program, were preparing to take their first swings at one another. After separating the two, Brandy was about to speak to the boys, when a voice came from behind. Seventeen-year-old Juwan, the leader and culture-setter of the group, calmly spoke, "Delon, my brother. This is a safe place. You can't hit other people and I won't let other people hit you."

This calmed both boys, along with the others who were watching. Ms. Brandy invited Jumari and Delon to walk to opposite ends of the gym and grab a drink. "Give it a couple minutes and when you're ready, jump back into the game." Almost as if nothing had happened, the rest of the boys kept playing.

Brandy smiled at Juwan, grateful for his leadership. He pointed to a small poster on the wall listing the club's "life scripts" which they reviewed at the beginning of every afternoon.

"This is a safe place, and I won't let anyone hit you you, so I can't let you hit because this is a safe place."[29]

An often neglected (but critically important) component of correcting bad behavior is to *proactively* teach appropriate behavior in calm moments. Life scripts are a powerful way to "proactively discipline."[30] We create an empowering environment with life scripts rather than a reactive one when undesirable behavior is displayed.

A handful of scripts, rehearsed consistently, go a long way in positively changing the environment and creating a safe, empowering place for *every* kid to work, play, and live together.

Known as "the law," the first five books of the Old Testament contain 613 prescriptive commands for the nation of Israel. Among those 613, nearly everyone has heard of the Ten Commandments.

Israel, God's chosen nation, was emerging from 400 years of slavery. Centuries of oppression led them to need to learn a new "script" for how to work, play, and live together. Their instincts, honed in captivity, needed recalibrating. The commandments—honor God, keep the Sabbath holy, don't kill, don't covet, honor you mother and father… are God's life scripts for His people.

Jesus would reframe the law into the life script of love.

> *Hearing that Jesus had silenced the Sadducees, the Pharisees got together. One of them, an expert in the law, tested him with this question: "Teacher, which is the greatest commandment in the Law?"*
>
> *Jesus replied: "'Love the Lord your God with all your heart and with all your soul and with all your mind.' This is the first and greatest commandment. And the second is like it: 'Love your neighbor as yourself.' All the Law and the Prophets hang on these two commandments."*
>
> — MATTHEW 22:34–40

Committing this teaching to memory is an important step to living the life Christ calls us to—a life of connection and peace—right in the midst of hurt and chaos.

Trauma—informed Tip

People who have experienced early childhood trauma often have trouble processing more than eight to twelve words at a time. Life scripts are a powerful and efficient way to redirect behavior using the fewest words necessary. In a calm and playful environment, teach life scripts like "With respect," "This is a safe place," or "Stick together, no hits, no hurts." Through role play, practice the positive behavior you expect to see when using each phrase so they become automatic during times of stress.

For more on life scripts, see Appendix A.

1. What phrases or sayings ("scripts") were a part of my household growing up? Did they bring me life or were they hurtful?
2. What are two or three truths from the Bible God wants me to use as "life scripts"? Memorize them.
3. What life scripts can I incorporate into a child's or teen's life? Is there a creative way to display them so that memorization is easy?

_____

_____

_____

_____

_____

_____

_____

_____

_____

_____

_____

_____

_____

_____

_____

_____

_____

_____

_____

_____

Prayer

Lord, Your words bring life and I want to have them in my mind and on my lips.
Help me commit them to memory and allow them to guide my actions. Amen.

This week, what did I learn about myself?
Others? The Lord?

A new commandment I give to you, that you love one another:
just as I have loved you, you also are to love one another.

— JOHN 13:34 (ESV) —

Week 8

How We Love Matters

The journey to becoming safe adults in the lives of vulnerable kids is a journey of learning to love well. We can learn to listen, to show up, to not intimidate or manipulate, to laugh, to play, to look for meaning behind behavior, and not to take bad behavior personally. We have the privilege of being someone who can tell a child,

"You are known. You are seen. You are loved."

In this final week, we will learn how to make it right when relationships break, to celebrate small beginnings, and to care for ourselves. This 40-day journey has provided guidance in loving Jesus, ourselves, and those around us even more.

Make It Right

So then let us pursue what makes for peace and for mutual upbuilding.
— ROMANS 14:19 (ESV)

Fifteen-year-old Sam sat quietly, taking in the harsh words of his foster dad, Matt. "You always do this, going behind our backs to get what you want! How many times do we have to have this conversation? Go to your room, and we'll talk about this later."

Matt hadn't given Sam the chance to speak. If he would have listened, Sam could have explained the new backpack was given to him by his soccer coach; it came with the new uniform. He didn't steal it, didn't ask for it, and wasn't trying to get around their plan for him to practice saving money. It just *happened*.

Now Matt was mad, and Sam was alone.

Matt hadn't meant to lose his temper. It had been a long day at work and when he saw Sam sitting there with the new backpack, the anger he managed to reign in all day bubbled over. Playing the scene back in his mind, he knew he was wrong. They had been working hard to connect with Sam, teaching him adults can be trusted. He blew it—over a backpack. His gut told him he should apologize, but wouldn't that undermine him as the parent? Weren't adults supposed to have it together? But then again, what about treating others the way he would want to be treated? Does that apply to disobedient foster sons?

The list of questions did nothing to ease Matt's conscience, and, after calming down, he decided to make things right, even if it meant admitting his mistakes. Sam barely acknowledged Matt's presence when he found him in his room, only taking out one headphone. The canyon of disconnection stretched between them, the months of bridge building broken.

"I'm sorry I lost my temper. I shouldn't have yelled. I had a rough day at work, and I took it out on you. Sometimes I'm going to mess up too. Will you forgive me?"

Today, Matt and Sam consider that the day their relationship shifted. On the other side of the apology, their relationship strengthened.

- Sam saw a powerful model of how to own mistakes and make them right.
- Matt experienced freedom from the expectation that, as the parent, he will always get it right.

Psychologists refer to mending our relational mistakes as "ruptures and repairs." Ruptures in relationships are unavoidable—the result of conflict and disagreement. Repair is optional. However, when relationships are repaired, a positive neurotransmitter called dopamine is released in the brain, strengthening neurological connections and physically building new ones. When we choose to repair ruptured relationships, it not only heals what's been broken, it makes the relationship—and connections in our brains—even stronger.

Healthy relationships are essential to a healthy life and will always require the hard work of repair. In the Sermon on the Mount, Jesus directly addresses what to do if we find ourselves in the middle of a rupture.

"This is how I want you to conduct yourself in these matters. If you enter your place of worship and, about to make an offering, you suddenly remember a grudge a friend has against you, abandon your offering, leave immediately, go to this friend and make things right. Then and only then, come back and work things out with God."

— MATTHEW 5:23–24 (MSG)

These are our instructions as followers of Jesus: *make things right.* The "friend" Jesus is referring to may be your coworker, spouse, neighbor, child, or teen. As Paul would later write to the church in Rome,

If possible, as far as it depends on you, live at peace with everyone.

— ROMANS 12:18 (CSB)

The call to repair ruptures is for everyone. This is the hard but fruitful work of living out the Gospel.

Trauma-informed Tip

When working with children and teens from hard places, look for opportunities to repair ruptured relationships. Rather than be discouraged by disconnection, use it as a teachable moment by modeling what it looks like to own your mistakes and make things right. When you do, you'll find the relationship stronger on the other side.

1. Do I need to repair a rupture with anyone?
2. Why might it be important to Jesus we live reconciled with others?
3. Has someone in my life modeled this before? If so, how did it make me feel to experience their vulnerability in asking for forgiveness? If not, how could that person pursuing a repair have improved our relationship?

_____

_____

_____

_____

_____

_____

_____

_____

_____

_____

_____

_____

_____

_____

_____

_____

_____

_____

_____

_____

Prayer

*God, You model so well how to maintain and pursue relationship.
I want to repair, restore, rebuild, reconcile, and live and look
like one of Your kids. Help me do this. Amen.*

Small Beginnings

And though your beginning was small, your latter days will be very great.
— JOB 8:7 (ESV)

As she walked out of the principal's office for the third time that week, Selma sighed, defeated. Despite her best efforts, no amount of encouragement, coaching, reward, or consequence could make her nine-year-old daughter, Ella, behave at school. Nearly every day was some version of the same story. Ella stole a classmate's snack. Ella threw her notebook at the teacher. Ella stood on the chair and dumped her pencils on the ground. Last week had been a good week, only one bad report, so Selma thought they were making progress. But *everything* with Ella felt like two steps forward, one step back.

With so much negativity at school, Selma knew she and Ella needed something positive to connect over at home. She pulled a few old garden pots out of the garage, found seed packets in a drawer, and grabbed a partial bag of soil. Together they planted the seeds and labeled each pot.

As weeks went by, Ella's behavior at school didn't show much improvement. But regardless of how the day went, Selma and Ella would tend their garden together. Ella was overjoyed as the first shoots began to push above the surface. She squealed with excitement the day the first flower bloomed and couldn't believe when a tiny tomato made its debut.

One night after watering her beloved plants, Ella put her hands on her hips, gazed up at Selma and said, "A lot of people at school don't think I'm good at anything, but if they could see my plants, they would know I am actually good at taking care of things."

Selma realized Ella was right. She *was* good at taking care of things. She followed instructions, waited patiently, and used her words to ask for help. These were all new skills. Selma had nearly missed these signs of healing. Just because there is a step backward, doesn't mean progress isn't being made. Selma and Ella celebrated together how their gardening helped them see things differently.

The path to healing is often long, slow, and winding. Most healing happens below the surface where we can't see it. Just like seeds planted into the darkness of the soil, growth needs time to show progress. The key is to look for glimmers of hope, or, as the prophet Zechariah would call them, small beginnings.

> *Do not despise these small beginnings, for the Lord rejoices to see the work begin.*
> — ZECHARIAH 4:10 (NLT)

The Lord *rejoices* in small beginnings, and we can too.

- When kids use their voice to ask for what they need, we rejoice!
- When they help a friend who is hurting, we rejoice!
- When they ask for a compromise, we rejoice!

Sometimes we see the end of the story—the beautiful fruit hanging off a tree we were a part of planting. But more often, we are called to be faithful planters or waterers, trusting God will give growth in His time.

> *So neither he who plants nor he who waters is anything,*
> *but only God who gives the growth.*
> — 1 CORINTHIANS 3:6–9 (ESV)

Sometimes the stories we are a part of bear fruit in later generations, long after we're gone. There is a tree that grows in Israel called the tamarisk tree. It doesn't fully bloom for sixty years, yet Abraham planted one.

Abraham planted a tamarisk tree in Beersheba and
called there on the name of the Lord, the Everlasting God.

— GENESIS 21:33

This man, who had yet to see God's promises fulfilled, was determined to prepare for what he believed would still come. He planted that tree for the benefit of future generations.

Let us rejoice in the planting and watering, in glimmers of hope, and in a God who is faithful to fulfill his promises to every generation.

Look for small milestones to celebrate. When you see a child or teen use a new skill like giving care, receiving care, or negotiating their needs, stop and recognize this as a small victory. Praise them by specifically acknowledging the task. Say something like, "That was a great job using good words to ask for what you need!" or "I saw you help your friend on the playground. That was really good taking care of others!" This will help you both recognize the small advances they are making.

1. What do I know God is growing in me, even if I can't see the full fruit yet? How can I thank Him for this work?
2. How am I currently "planting a tamarisk tree"—a seed that won't bear fruit right away but will bless later generations?
3. What simple ways can I "water" those around me, trusting God will grow them?

Prayer

Jesus, nothing is unnoticed to You. You see and measure completely differently than we do. Help me to be faithful and obedient. Amen.

In Him All Things Hold Together

And rising very early in the morning, while it was still dark,
he departed and went out to a desolate place, and there he prayed.

— MARK 1:35 (ESV)

Jen reviews the list again: laundry, meeting at school, basketball practice, grocery shopping, birthday gift for mom, casserole for the church potluck... It feels like her to-do list will never end. Her phone buzzes on the bedside table before she even opens her eyes. A neighbor's mom has died, and she'll need to make them a meal. *So much for my doctor's appointment this afternoon.* It will wait until next month. It's already been six months since the pain in her side began, so what's one more?

Derrick loves his job at the Youth Center, helping kids live up to their potential and follow their dreams. It's his passion, his calling. He doesn't even care how much overtime he puts in, because the kids are worth it. Most nights he arrives home around 11:00 p.m., since he stays to make sure everyone has a ride. Then he's out the door by 4:00 a.m., making rounds to get everyone to school. It's a little exhausting, but if he doesn't do it, *who will?*

Marie was so excited when she received the call to fill an emergency placement as a caregiver to seven boys. She envisioned family dinners, soccer games, and birthday parties. What she hadn't anticipated were temper tantrums, fist fights, and constant rejection. Just three months in, she's already forgetting what life was like before. She used to love to cook, spend time with friends, and read her Bible each morning. There isn't time for any of that anymore. She wonders, *Is this the price of serving God?*

Jen, Derrick, and Marie are all walking the same path. It begins with good intentions, a big heart, and an abundance of compassion but ends with resentment, bitterness, and burnout. They care deeply for others but aren't caring well for themselves.

Self-care refers to the activities and practices we engage in on a regular basis to reduce stress and enhance our health and well-being. Self-care is what allows us to sustain the hard work of loving and caring for children who have experienced trauma. It's not a reward, and it isn't selfish. It's *good stewardship* of the body, mind, and soul we have been given.

Throughout His earthly ministry, Jesus modeled healthy rhythms of self-care.

* Jesus took care of Himself *physically*. He took naps, rested, and walked.
* Jesus took care of Himself *emotionally*. He knew solitude was needed, and He withdrew from the crowds even as they clamored to see him.
* Jesus took care of Himself *socially*. He ate with and sought the company of friends.
* Jesus took care of Himself *spiritually*. He regularly spent time alone with the Father.

When Jesus needed food or water, He asked for it. When Jesus needed emotional support from his friends, He didn't hide it. When Jesus' heart was broken, He wept. Jesus was faithful to God, and part of faithfulness was taking care of His real human needs. No one denies Jesus' life included suffering and sacrifice, *yet it did not include self-neglect or self-destruction.* He cared for Himself, knowing this was the only way He could complete the work He was put on the earth to accomplish.

Jesus, being fully divine yet fully human, found self-care to be not only helpful, but necessary. Why are we so quick to assume we don't need it too?

It's easy to find ourselves believing we are the ones who must hold all things together. Jesus' example invites us to remember it is in *Him* all things hold together (Colossians 1:17). If Jesus unapologetically took time to rest and to care for Himself, we can too.

Trauma-informed Tip

Take time to reflect on your current self-care practices. Identify areas of strength and areas of weakness. Then create one new goal for self-care. For example, increase physical self-care by taking a walk three times a week or increase social care by asking someone for coffee or dinner. If you are prone to creating unrealistic expectations for yourself and then feeling the shame of failure, set micro goals—short attainable targets that create momentum towards a healthier lifestyle.

Take stock with these questions:

1. How am I caring for myself physically? Am I eating healthy, getting exercise, and seeking routine medical care?
2. How am I caring for myself emotionally? Am I taking time to reflect, grieve, and receive wise counsel?
3. How am I caring for myself socially? Am I talking with friends, sharing meals, and visiting new places?
4. How am I caring for myself spiritually? Am I gathering with other believers, reading God's Word, and spending time in prayer?
5. In which area of self-care am I lacking and which comes most naturally to me?
6. What does it say about Jesus that He also took care of himself? Where can I find an example in Scripture of Him doing so?

_____

_____

_____

_____

_____

_____

_____

_____

_____

_____

_____

_____

_____

_____

_____

_____

_____

_____

_____

_____

_____

Prayer

Jesus, I know I need better self-care. Help me to be honest, find good rhythm, and be open to accountability. I want to grow and be healthy. Amen.

The Trauma-informed Life

Because you are precious in my eyes, and honored, and I love you.

— ISAIAH 43:4 (ESV)

In the same way Jesus said the world would recognize his disciples by the way they love one another, there are specific characteristics that make a trauma-informed person recognizable.

- **Jesus understood the life-altering impact of trauma.**
  He was there in the beginning—the creation of Eden. He understands the wholeness Adam and Eve experienced in His presence. He was also there when it all fell apart and knows how far we are from the goodness and beauty intended in the garden. We can't engage fully in His ministry without understanding and accepting this truth.

In the beginning was the Word, and the Word was with God, and the Word was God. He was with God in the beginning. Through him all things were made; without him nothing was made that has been made.

— JOHN 1:1–3

- **Jesus viewed life through the lens of the wounded.**
  As he lived his life on Earth, Jesus experienced pain, hardship, and loss. Jesus wept and Jesus was wounded. He spent his time with the sinner and the outcast. He knew their stories and how their woundedness colored their views of the world. Jesus understood what it means to be wounded. We are called to view life through the same lens, trusting that His woundedness brings healing and being the living example of that to the wounded around us.

But he was pierced for our transgressions; he was crushed for our iniquities, upon him was the chastisement that brought us peace, and with his wounds we are healed.

— ISAIAH 53:5

- **Jesus didn't offer a "one size fits all" healing.**
  He knew the distinct brokenness of each person He encountered and the unique method He would use to restore wholeness. Jesus wasn't limited to one pathway of healing, and we should be on the lookout for individualized ways we can extend His healing to others.

  - He healed with words (Matthew 9:6–7).
  - He healed through touch (Matthew 20:34).
  - He healed through his garment (Matthew 9:20–22).
  - He healed with clay (John 9:6).
  - He healed with his own saliva (Mark 8:22–25).

- **Jesus managed his own emotional response.**
  Being fully human, Jesus experienced a full range of emotions. He was heartbroken over the death of his friend Lazarus, angry at the hypocrisy of religious leaders, disgusted by the greed on display in the temple courts, and pained in His rejection. Yet still He did not sin when suffering attacks on his character, identity, and validity. Trauma-informed helpers don't deny their own emotional pain, but refuse to be controlled by it.

He committed no sin, neither was deceit found in his mouth. When he was reviled, he did not revile in return; when he suffered, he did not threaten, but continued entrusting himself to him who judges justly.

— 1 PETER 2:22–23

- **Jesus accepted help.**

  He looked to his Father for guidance, accepted five loaves and two fishes from a young boy, and used the home of a certain man to celebrate the Passover. He leaned on his disciples for companionship and accepted the comfort of angels in the hours before his final arrest and death. We deny the reality of Christ in us if we deny our need for help—from Him *and* from others He puts in our path.

- **Jesus knew the past impacts the present.**

  When Jesus spoke with the woman at the well, it was His knowledge of her past she later testified to.

  > *Many Samaritans from that town believed in him because*
  > *of the woman's testimony, "He told me all that I ever did."*
  >
  > — JOHN 4:39

  Jesus was unafraid to address the past and ultimately will use our broken stories to work all things for good. Testifying to our own stories of healing allows others to imagine it for themselves.

Jesus modeled a trauma-informed life in how He loved and lived. May it be our life's journey to live and love like He does.

Trauma-informed Tip

- **Understand the life-altering impact of trauma**. Learn to recognize trauma and its effects.
- **View life through the lens of a wounded child**. Put on the lens of a wounded child and work at seeing life from their perspective.
- **Understand there is no "one size fits all" approach to healing**. Be willing to set aside preconceived ideas of how to parent or give care to a child.
- **Know how to manage your own emotions**. Know there will be challenges to you personally. Prepare for those challenges by learning to manage your own emotional responses.
- **Ask for help**. Be willing to admit you don't have all the answers or cannot do this alone. You will need to be open and vulnerable to others.
- **Be aware of how the past impacts the present.** Take time to process not only the personal histories of others but also your own personal history.

---

1. Who in my life acts like Jesus by living out these qualities? How can I thank them for loving me like Jesus does?
2. Where, how, or with whom is God calling me to implement the things I have learned in this study?
3. What is one way I can become even more trauma-informed? What is my next step?

Prayer

Jesus, I want to look like You. I want to serve, parent, minister, and be like You. I need Your strength and wisdom. I ask You for it. Amen.

Now Go

*God is not unjust; he will not forget your work and the love you
have shown him as you have helped his people and continue to help them*

— HEBREWS 6:10

"You can't lead a child to a place you've never been."

— DR. KARYN PURVIS

Most of us seek information regarding trauma principles, so we can be more compassionate and effective while working with children. Routinely, the surprise is when it uncovers places in our own stories where restoration and reconciliation is required. If this is you, the journey of healing is hard, but worth taking. Find someone to journey with you as you understand more about how your history affects the present and your relationships.

The principles outlined in this devotional can be used in every area of life.
- They can make us more effective listeners.
- They can make us more sensitive partners.
- They can improve our parenting, even for children without a trauma history.
- They can open our eyes to spiritual truths and remind us that...

He who began a good work in you will carry it on to completion until the day of Christ Jesus

— PHILIPPIANS 1:6

Hopefully you've fallen more in love with Jesus through these forty days as you've seen how He offers restoration and reconciliation to the wounded, which includes everyone. Now is the moment to commit to continued growth and healing as a person. "Trauma competency" doesn't change children, it changes the adult who

interacts with children. God loves us more than He wants to use us, so continue the good work He has begun in you. He wants us to experience healing and freedom. That's what will spill over into the calling He has for each of us.

Putting a new skill into practice requires discipline. We *can* act as agents of healing in the lives of children, but like everything else in our journey of discipleship, it won't be easy and will require consistent time and effort. Now armed with tools and understanding, let's come together as a community to encourage one another towards healing.

The best news is we are only the conduits of God's goodness to children. We will never have everything we need to parent/coach/teach/lead a child who has experienced a traumatic history. As we go to God for patience, self-control, wisdom, discernment, joy, kindness… or whatever we are lacking, He will provide through His Spirit everything we need.

Trauma-informed Tip

Take at least one of these next steps:

- Make a commitment to a child, a program that serves children, or an organization that you trust is caring for children in healing ways. There's not much we can do about the statistics indicating one billion children are traumatized, but investing in and influencing even one life makes a difference.

- Ask God with whom you can share your new understanding. Teaching someone the new insights you've gained will reinforce what you've learned and may inspire that person to embark on their own journey.

- Take a moment to honestly review how you've interacted with those who have a trauma history. Is there a situation where you wish you could have a re-do? Ask God for forgiveness, remembering the grace He offers is free to all who ask. If appropriate, ask forgiveness from those you might have hurt. Don't demand or even expect it, but it could spur on healing for them.

- Consider further training. We recommend Trauma Free World's courses, but wherever and however you get started, recognize this as a lifelong journey.

Thank you for being on this journey with us. As you've learned from our families and stories, we pray you've gained understanding to apply in the lives of children around you.

Prayer

Jesus, we want to do Your will. We want to heal. We want to give away the love You've given us. Help us to have eyes to see. Amen.

This week, what did I learn about myself?
Others? The Lord?

Life Value Scripts

One of the main tasks of safe adults is to coach children in appropriate life values and social skills. Life value scripts are short phrases taught proactively, then later used to redirect behavior.

Tips for Using Life Scripts

1. **Teach through play.** Scripts should be taught and practiced when the child and adult are calm, regulated, and connected.

2. **Stick to the script.** When correcting behavior, it's easy to want to add extra words. Remember, in a moment of dysregulation, a child can comprehend very few words. Repeat the script in a calm and affirming manner.

3. **Find what works for you.** Adapt the exact phrasing of scripts to your context. All scripts should honor relationships and teach social skills but can be adapted to fit your specific environment.

Sample Scripts

No hits, no hurts.

Be kind and gentle.

Ask permission.

With respect.

Listen and obey.

Asking or telling?

Stick together.

Keep your promise.

Wait to speak.

I will listen.

Use your words.

Adapted from Purvis, K. B. , Ph. D. , Cross, D. R. , Ph. D. , & Sunshine, W. L. (2007). The Connected Child: Bring Hope and Healing to Your Adoptive Family. New York: McGraw-Hill, p. 74.

LEARN MORE

Training teaches us how to help ourselves and each other find a brighter path.

Learn more about how to love, work and live in a trauma-informed way. Use coupon code PRESENCE for one free on-demand class.

traumafreeworld.org

TRAUMA
FREE
WORLD

Acknowledgements

This project came together as a result of the combined efforts of Rob Hall, Samantha Mathews, Jenna Ghizas, Steph Duff, and Alex Moore. They gathered stories, brainstormed trauma tips, researched the science, studied Scripture, edited the latest draft, and created questions. I am so grateful to be on a team of dedicated, passionate Christ followers who love the vulnerable child.

I also want to acknowledge the Back2Back Ministries and Trauma Free World teams who work daily to serve children. Their stories are insightful and their drive to be constant learners and excellent at what they do is inspiring! I am thankful to co-labor alongside you.

Thank you to Paul Coty, for believing in this message. I'm grateful for the calls and encouragement to get this resource out. Thank you to David Henriksen and the whole iDisciple team. Your professionalism and commitment to the project made me constantly sing your praise.

Finally, I want to acknowledge David and Jayne Schooler. When you found us, we were committed but uninformed in the best practices of working with children who have a trauma history. You trained a few, and then us all, helping to take this message now to more than 76 countries, representing nearly 1,100 organizations. I pray you see your work and passion multiplied in those being trained in trauma-informed care.

1. Perry, B. D., Pollard, R. A., Blakley, T. L., Baker, W. L., & Vigilante, D. (1995). Childhood trauma, the neurobiology of adaptation, and "use-dependent" development of the brain: How "states" become "traits." *Infant Mental Health Journal, 16*(4), 217-291.

2. Burke-Harris, N. (2018). *The Deepest Well.* Simon & Schuster.

3. Ibid.

4. International Society for Traumatic Stress Studies. (2016). [Pamplet]. Trauma and Relationships.

5. Kisiel C., Pauter S., Ocampo A., Stokes C., Bruckner E. (2021). Trauma-informed guiding principles for working with transition age youth: Provider fact sheet. Los Angeles, CA and Durham, NC: National Center for Child Traumatic Stress.

6. Back2Back Ministries. (2019). Trauma Competent Caregiver Training.

7. The Alert Program. See https://www.alertprogram.com/product/alert-program-how-does-your-engine-run/

8. Fiese, B. H., Thomas, J. T., Douglas, M., Josephs, K., Plotrock, S., & Baker, T. A review of 50 years of research on naturally occurring family routines and rituals: Cause for celebration? *Journal of Family Psychology, 16*(4).

9. Siegel, D. & Sroufe, A. (2011, March/April). The verdict is in: The case for attachment theory. *Psychotherapy Networker.*

10. Maté, D. G., & Neufeld, G. (2006). *Hold on to your kids: Why parents need to matter more than peers*. Vermillion.

11. Ibid.

12. Cassidy, J. (2001). Truth, lies, and intimacy: An attachment perspective. *Attachment & Human Development, 3*(2), 121-155. DOI: 10.1080/14616730110058999

13. Perry, B. D., Pollard, R. A., Blakley, T. L., Baker, W. L., & Vigilante, D. (1995). Childhood trauma, the neurobiology of adaptation, and "use-dependent" development of the brain: How "states" become "traits." *Infant Mental Health Journal, 16*(4), 217-291.

14. Back2Back Ministries. (2019). Trauma Competent Caregiver Training.

15. Schultz, N. (2007, May 31). Fetuses experience stress earlier than thought. *New Scientist*. https://www. newscientist.com/article/dn11960-fetuses-experience-stress-earlier-than-thought/

16. Siegel, D. J., & Bryson, T. (2012). *The whole-brain child: 12 revolutionary strategies to nurture your child's developing mind*. Bantam Books.

17. Siegel, D. J., & Hartzell, M. (2018). *Parenting from the inside out: How a deeper self-understanding can help you raise children who thrive*. Scribe Publications.

18. Purvis, K., Cross, D., & Sunshine, W. L. (2007). *The connected child: Bring hope and healing to your adoptive family.* McGraw-Hill.

19. Bath, H. (2008). Three pillars of trauma-informed care. *Reclaiming Children and Youth, 17*(3), 17-21.

20. Bowlby, J. (1973). *Attachment and loss. Vol. 2. Separation: Anxiety and anger.* Basic Books.

21. Bernier, A., Carlson, S. & Whipple, N. (2010). From external regulation to self-regulation: Early parenting precursors of young children's executive functioning. *Child Development, 81*(1), 326-339.

22. King, T. S., Toney, G. M., Tian, P. & Javors, M. A. (2011). Dehydration increases sodium-dependent glutamate uptake by hypothalamic paraventricular nucleus synaptosomes, *Neuro Endocrinol Lett. 32*(6), 763-768.

23. Jiang, X., Ma, H., Wang, Y. & Liu, Y. (2013). Early life factors and Type 2 Diabetes Mellitus, *J Diabetes Res.*

24. Martinelli, K. (n.d.) Why do kids have trouble with transitions? Child Mind Institute. https://childmind.org/article/why-do-kids-have-trouble-with-transitions/

25. National Child Traumatic Stress Network. (2014). Trauma-Informed Principles.

26. Karyn Purvis Institute of Child Development. (2011). Trust-Based Parenting [Video file]. Texas Christian University.

27. Perry, B. D., Pollard, R. A., Blakley, T. L., Baker, W. L., & Vigilante, D. (1995). Childhood trauma, the neurobiology of adaptation, and "use-dependent" development of the brain: How "states" become "traits." *Infant Mental Health Journal, 16*(4), 217-291.

28. Spera, C. (2005, June). A review of the relationship among parenting practices, parenting styles, and adolescent school achievement. *Educational Psychology Review, 17*(2). DOI: 10.1007/s10648-005-3950-1

29. Vicario, M. (1986). *Safety script: How to build felt safety in ourselves, those around us, and our environment.* Finding Hope Consulting, LLC.

30. Siegel, D. J., & Hartzell, M. (2018). *Parenting from the inside out: How a deeper self-understanding can help you raise children who thrive.* Scribe Publications.